BALANCING
IT ALL

New York Times Best-selling Author

BALANCING IT ALL

My Story of Juggling Priorities and Purpose

CANDACE CAMERON BURE

WITH DANA WILKERSON

Nashville, Tennessee

I dedicate this book to my family, friends, and fans.
Without you, I wouldn't have as much to balance!
I love you all!

Acknowledgments

From Candace:

I'd like to thank Jennifer Lyell for believing that I'm more than a one-hit wonder. It's because of your encouragement, enthusiasm, and insight that I was able draw out the practical truths of my life and use them as a witnessing opportunity. You saw in me what I couldn't see myself. I am blessed to have you as my editor and friend.

Dana Wilkerson, there's nothing like being thrown together and getting to know each other really quickly! I couldn't have done this without you. Thank you for all your hard work and efforts. You are a superstar!

Mom and Dad, you've been my rock-solid example when it comes to family. You've continued a generational legacy with your commitment to one another through good times and difficult ones. Thank you for being an example of a godly marriage. I love you with all my heart.

I'd also like to thank Jeffery Brooks and Ford Englerth for effortlessly handling all the details including my vision for the cover shoot. Thank you to Tara Brooks, Rowan Daly, and Juliet Vo. My sincerest thanks to B&H Publishing for your continued support and trust. Thank you to everyone including my Twitter and Facebook followers who prayed for me through this book, with a special shout-out to Stacy W.

To my beautiful family, thank you for your patience, love, and support when you see your wife and mom stare at a computer screen for countless hours at weeks on end. I can't promise it won't happen again. And to my Lord and Savior, Jesus Christ, to You all glory is given; for it wasn't me who did a thing, but You who sacrificed it all and created me with a heart's desire to know You, follow You, and freely accept Your love, mercy, and grace.

From Dana:

Candace, working with you has been a joy. It was a fast, roller-coaster ride, but well worth it. Thanks for all of the prayers, hard work, and late nights!

Jennifer, as always it has been a pleasure partnering with you on this book. Thank you for your support, trust, and friendship.

Mom and Dad, thank you for your unconditional love, for being such great examples for me, and for showing me what it means to live a full and balanced life. I wouldn't be the woman I am today without you!

Chad, Beth, Maura, Claire, and Nicholas, thanks for your undying support and for providing me with such a great home-away-from-home.

I also want to thank many other friends and family members who have prayed for me and been patient with me as I've worked on this book: the Baugh & Dunn clan; Amanda, Ashley, Nicole, Zack, and many others at Osage Hills; as well as Heidi, Holley, Jenny, and Vicki. You all are the best!

Most of all, I want to thank my Lord and Savior, Jesus Christ, without whom none of this would be possible!

Contents

Introduction

S o you think I've got it all figured out? If you read anything about me or from me online, it may seem like I have no trouble balancing family life, work, my social life, church, and everything else I do. I realize it could seem perfectly joyful and balanced when you read my tweets or see my Facebook updates. "Candace, you're my role model," women respond. Or, "Your faithfulness is so inspiring!" I also get a lot of, "You're such a great mom." And then there's, "I want to be just like you!" The compliments may feel good, but many days I feel like all I'm really good at is fooling everybody!

If you were to see me on the street and ask, "What are your top priorities?" my immediate response would be, "God and family." In fact, many people say their priorities are, in order: (1) God, (2) family, (3) work. That sounds great, but it's not really a hierarchy, and priorities are more complicated than that. As a Christian, my love for and obedience to

God should permeate all else. So He's not the top priority, He's the ultimate priority and is a part of everything I do. Throughout this book if it seems that I'm not repeating the fact that God is or should be my "top priority," it's because that's a given for me as a Christian. In all that I do, I strive to do what God would have me do.

I also find that my family is—or can be—an aspect of many of the other priorities in my life. For instance, I work to help financially support my family. And my choice to live a healthy life directly impacts everyone in my home—both because it also causes them to live in a healthy manner and because when I'm healthy it helps me to better take care of my kids and husband.

With the exception of God and family, I find that the expression of most of my other priorities will change in importance from day to day, from week to week, and throughout the different stages of my life. When I think about this, I am reminded of Ecclesiastes 3:1–8:

> For everything there is a season, and a time for
>   every matter under heaven:
> a time to be born, and a time to die;
> a time to plant, and a time to pluck up what is
>   planted;
> a time to kill, and a time to heal;
> a time to break down, and a time to build up;
> a time to weep, and a time to laugh;

a time to mourn, and a time to dance;
a time to cast away stones, and a time to gather
　　stones together;
a time to embrace, and a time to refrain from
　　embracing;
a time to seek, and a time to lose;
a time to keep, and a time to cast away;
a time to tear, and a time to sew;
a time to keep silence, and a time to speak;
a time to love, and a time to hate;
a time for war, and a time for peace.

No two days, weeks, years, or seasons of anyone's life look exactly the same. Some things stay the same, but our lives are constantly changing. We need to be open to those changes and be willing to reorder and balance our lives as necessary.

If you're like me, sometimes it seems as if life isn't so much a balancing act as a juggling act. There are so many things going on that I just can't manage to hold onto all of them at once. When this happens, I just remember that I need to reprioritize and reevaluate every single day. I also remind myself that I can't do it on my own—I need God's help, as well as the help of my husband, kids, and other people in my life to make it all happen and pick up the slack.

As you think about how to balance your life and prioritize the many parts of it, I want you to remember that your priorities are *your* priorities—no one else's. You are unique and your situation is unique. So while it's wise to look at others' choices, don't copy them exactly or compare yourself to them. They have different people in their lives, different situations, and different resources. Along that same vein, don't expect others to prioritize their lives the same way you do.

Before we get started, I want to acknowledge that some people might say that the easiest way to create balance in our lives is to strip our commitments down to the bare minimum. You're going to see that is definitely not my message. Instead, I think balance is achieved when we are well rounded and focusing on all the things God has created us to be and do. That is when our priorities will most clearly overlap and it is through that overlap that balance is most natural. So, yes, this is a book about balance, but you'll see that it's about understanding principles that help identify what I've learned to prioritize in life. And through those priorities, I've learned the value of balance—even though I don't always master it!

As you read this book, consider the principles found among the pages, but don't try to model your life exactly after mine. At the same time, try not to discount the things I say or do simply because you think I can't relate to you due to our different lives and experiences. Remember that you are unique. Your life is different than mine, so the precise way you balance and prioritize the parts of your life will be different than the way I do it, but we can all learn from the principles we see in each other's choices.

I hope you'll learn from my stories, the good and the bad. I'm not superwoman. I'm just another working mom and wife trying to balance, juggle, and maintain this twenty-first-century life, living it to the fullest, with conviction and morals, trying to live it well. Warning: There will be some spilled milk and broken smart phones along the way, but if we're in it together, we will find our joy!

Blessings,
Candace

CHAPTER 1

Monkey See, Monkey Do

Train up a child in the way he should go;
even when he is old he will not depart from it.
—Proverbs 22:6

• • • • • • • • • • • • •

What would you like for your birthday, Maks?" Val and I asked our youngest before his seventh birthday. His response: "All I want to do is play hockey. Please, Papa? Please? I wanna be a hockey player just like you!" Ugh, three years of skirting the issue finally came to a sudden halt. How could we resist those big, blue, hopeful eyes? How could we resist the one and only request for his birthday? Maks had been begging to play hockey since he was four years old and Val had been pushing his hardest to turn our kids into tennis players. Players can get injured in any sport, but hockey can be extremely brutal. After six concussions and multiple knee, shoulder, elbow, hip, and back surgeries, Val would do everything in his power to steer our boys clear of hockey life. I mean, come on, tennis could be played in the sunshine, outdoors, on clay and grass—surfaces not nearly as hard and cold as rock-solid ice. But as life would have it, our boys were destined to play hockey, and not without Dad as their head coach.

"Do what I say, not what I do." How many times have you heard parents say that to their kids? Probably a lot. And how many times do the kids do what the parents say instead of what they do? Likely none. The truth is, when it comes to children, "monkey see, monkey do" is the name of the game. Even from a young age, kids will do what they see their parents doing, and without some form of intervention they'll likely continue those patterns throughout their lives.

As a parent, I have to remember that I am constantly teaching my children, whether I want to—or realize I'm doing it—or not. Though I believe it is important to tell my kids how their dad and I want them to live and behave, the primary means of teaching is through action. If we live the way we want our kids to live, there's a good chance they'll pick up on it. When we purposefully live balanced lives and strive to prioritize in the ways God wants us to, our kids will see, experience, and emulate that without even knowing it's happening.

One of the reasons I am able to balance my life and keep my priorities in line is because of the example my parents set for me. Thinking back to what I learned from them, I consider how important it is to create balanced lives for my own children. I am so grateful for my parents' influence in my life and the lives of my three siblings. Were they perfect parents? No. No one is. But for the most part they strove to do what they believed was right, and I believe I am a better person for it.

Cameron Family Beginnings

Robert Cameron and Barbara Bausmith were married on June 22, 1969 (exactly twenty-seven years before my husband Val and I got married). Mom was barely out of high school, and Dad was a junior high math teacher. My brother Kirk was born in the fall of 1970, followed by my sister Bridgette eleven months later. Three years passed and my sister Melissa was born, and then on April 6, 1976, I rounded out the Cameron clan. Not long after my birth, my parents bought a modest home in Canoga Park, California, where they lived until November of 2012.

When Mom was growing up, her family went to church, but they were more focused on living a moral life than on living life for God. When Mom married Dad, she figured they'd raise their kids the same way. She was wrong . . . partly. Dad was very concerned with morality, but he wanted nothing to do with church or religion and didn't want his family involved. So my brother, sisters, and I did not grow up in a Christian home, but we were still taught biblical principles, though my dad wouldn't have called them that. My parents wanted us to be kind, respectful, responsible, and honest, and to treat others as we would want to be treated. They taught us that it was important to give to others who were less fortunate than us and to be aware of the "real" world outside our family. We were expected to know right from wrong and to be good, upstanding, moral citizens who worked hard at whatever we did.

My parents tell me that even as a young child I had a strong sense of right and wrong, even though I didn't always *do* what I knew was right. I also wanted to do things just the way Mom did, so I purposely picked up many of her traits, both good and bad. (Yet another reminder that our kids will do what we do!) One of the traits she sometimes regrets passing on to me is a love of carrot cake, apple fritters, and mint chocolate chip ice cream. I'll have to admit, that love of decadent foods has gotten both of us into some trouble over the years!

Though my parents weren't on the same page when it came to church attendance, they were in agreement on many of their child-rearing practices. They wanted us to be well-rounded kids with balanced lives. They encouraged after-school activities such as soccer and ballet, but they didn't overextend us in those activities. Mom and Dad were both determined that family was—and always would be—a top priority. Along with spending time together as a nuclear family, we also spent a lot of time with our grandparents, aunts, uncles, and cousins. During my childhood, my sisters were my best friends, and they remain some of my best friends to this day. During the first twelve years of my marriage I lived thousands of miles away from my family, and one of the best things about being back in California is that I have been able to see my parents, grandparents, siblings, nieces, and nephews on a regular basis, and my kids get to spend time with their extended family just like I did as a child.

Hollywood Hopefuls

For a short time after Bridgette was born, my parents lived in a little apartment where they had a neighbor named

Fran Rich. Mom and Fran really hit it off, and though Mom didn't know it at the time, that relationship would eventually change our lives in a drastic way. Some of you may have heard of Fran's son, Adam, who played Nicholas Bradford, the youngest son on the TV show *Eight Is Enough* in the late 1970s and early '80s. During the time when my parents lived by the Rich family in the early '70s, Adam appeared in many commercials. Fran thought Kirk and Bridgette would be perfect for commercials too, and tried to get Mom to take them to meet Adam's agent, but Mom wasn't interested. Her life was full enough as it was. She simply wanted to be with her children and raise them to be happy, respectful, and healthy individuals. She enjoyed being a stay-at-home mom and didn't want to complicate her life or her kids' lives. Considering her family was not yet complete, I believe she made a wise choice.

Fast-forward to my aunt's wedding when I was four years old. My siblings and I were all there and Mom took a lot of photos of us, as moms are prone to do. Mom showed some of the pictures to Fran, who once again told Mom she should talk to Adam's agent. Since the other kids were all in school and I was in preschool a few days a week, Mom wasn't as busy as she had been, so she agreed to let Fran send the photos to Iris Burton, who was then the biggest name in children's agents. Mom wasn't all that sure she was doing the right thing. It had never been her dream for us to be in show business, but since we lived in the right place, she agreed to give it a shot, as long as we were all willing. Needless to say, we were.

Iris agreed to see all four of us, so one day Mom dressed us all up and she and Dad took us to Iris's house. One at a time, she asked each of us to step forward and say a few lines as she directed. When we had all taken a turn, she agreed to take on Kirk and Melissa for one year. She said I was too young and could come back in a year and my sister Bridgette needed to wait until her braces were off.

So Mom began taking Kirk and Melissa on commercial auditions. She told the two of them—as she told me a year later—that if at any point they wanted to stop, they could. I don't have to tell you that Kirk and I didn't get to that point. But Melissa, after doing one commercial and nearly getting cast in a TV series, decided she no longer wanted to be in the industry. It didn't fit her personality; she wasn't comfortable in front of the camera.

When my siblings started going to auditions, Mom saw it as more of a temporary diversion than anything. It was fun to dream of what might be, but she really didn't think it would happen. After all, the vast majority of kids who try to break into the entertainment industry don't ever book one job, much less become a star.

Dad looked at it simply as an extracurricular activity that also happened to make us a little bit of money. While Mom secretly hoped we'd make it big, he never thought any of us would make a career of it. He wanted more security for his children's futures than what he thought acting would give us. He was determined that no matter what happened, we were all going to college so we would be able to support ourselves with a normal, respectable, well-paying job.

A New Balancing Act

With four kids—two of whom were in the entertainment industry—how did my parents balance it all? The quick answer is that they already had a lifestyle that was conducive to it. If they hadn't, Mom wouldn't have allowed Fran to send Iris our photos. It simply wouldn't have been an option, because my parents wouldn't have been able to make it work.

Dad was a teacher and Mom stayed at home, so they didn't have much money, but they did have time. Mom had the time to take Kirk and me to auditions and shoots, and Dad was able to take us to school and be home after school to take care of whichever kids weren't working that day. Dad also took care of things around the house when Mom was off with one of us in the evenings. He cooked, cleaned, did laundry, and helped with homework. But no matter what, we all ate dinner together every night. Mom and Dad allowed us to work, but family was still the top priority. They agreed if that ever changed and our work started to interfere with our family life, that would be it. They'd pull us out of the industry.

My mom learned early on that her top priorities when we were working were to protect us and keep us grounded in the midst of what was often chaos. By the time I started auditioning for commercials, Mom was an old pro. She was determined not to be a stage mom, and she was even more determined that we wouldn't become entitled Hollywood brats. She had seen a handful of both varieties and she wanted nothing to do with it. She also didn't want us to experience the dog-eat-dog Hollywood world, so she did all she could to protect us from it.

When we would go to auditions, we would enter the waiting area just long enough to pick up our sides (the lines we would have to say) and then we would go to a hallway or a far-off corner to practice. Oftentimes, the rooms were packed with moms combing their kids' hair while the kids rehearsed out loud where others could hear, or they were talking about the commercials and movies their kids had recently booked. Mom tried to stay out of that atmosphere as much as possible so we could enjoy the experience without feeling like our value lay in whether or not we had as many jobs as the other kids. She wanted us to be confident in ourselves and know that whether or not we booked a job, we walked away knowing we gave it our best effort. She would tell us, "Have lots of energy and be yourself. And remember, if you don't get the part, it's not because you weren't good. They were just looking for someone different than you."

As Kirk and I were working more and more, there came a time when we needed a manager. It wasn't difficult for my parents to agree that Mom would be best suited for that job. They could have hired someone, but Mom already had a lot of experience with the industry by this point, and they knew nobody else would have our best interests at heart the way Mom did. Why pay someone else to do what Mom was basically already doing.

I didn't realize it at the time, because I was so young and didn't know any different, but when I look back on it now, I'm so glad Mom and Dad made that choice. I have had professional managers since then, and they're fantastic, but I'm grateful that it was Mom who had the opportunity to shape my character and my career. Nobody else could have done it as well as she did, because nobody else would have put my needs and interests before their own.

When I was in third grade, Kirk was cast in *Growing Pains*. If you ask my mom, I'm sure she'd say that life became a little more chaotic when that happened. However, for me life didn't seem crazy at all, which is a testament to my parents' ability to balance our lives and keep our priorities where they should be. But even in the chaos, my parents still kept the focus on family. One of my favorite times of the week was Friday night, which was tape night for *Growing Pains*. We'd all head to the studio to be part of the live audience for the show. If the taping didn't go too late, we'd go out to eat afterward with any other friends or family members who had attended the taping with us. It was all about family for us, and the same is true of my family today. Even though our lives are sometimes hectic, we make it a point to spend a lot of quality time together. We do not let the chaos intrude upon the areas of life that are more important.

Train Up a Child

The Bible tells us in Proverbs 22:6: "Train up a child in the way he should go; even when he is old he will not depart from it." I definitely don't consider myself to be "old," but I can honestly say that I have not departed from what my parents taught me through both word and action when I was a child. I have added to what they taught me, through studying God's Word and learning what it means to follow Him, but they created a good foundation.

My parents not only taught me to be a moral person, to treat others the way I want to be treated, and to know right from wrong, but they also taught me how to be a good parent and to guide a child in the direction and way I believe is right. Again, my Christian faith has greatly added to my understanding of parenting, but I often make family and parenting decisions partly based on what I experienced and observed from my own parents as a child. This is a great reminder to me that I need to be the godly parent God wants me to be so that in time, my kids can also be godly parents. They will be much more strongly positioned to parent in the same way I do, and I want that to be a good example, for their sake and the sake of my future grandchildren.

Note that the proverb I quoted says "a child," not "your child." Whether you do or don't have children of your own, I'm sure you have other kids that look up to you. Maybe you have nieces or nephews or friends' children that you love and spend a lot of time with. Perhaps you coach youth sports or teach kids at school, at church, or as a tutor. Even though you're not their parent, they're watching you too. They pick up on how you treat them, how you talk about and interact with others, how you spend your time, what your priorities are, and so on. There's a chance that you are a more positive role model for those kids than their own parents are. If that's the case, I want to challenge you to take your relationship with those children seriously and recognize the influence you can have not just over the way they live their lives now, but also how they will conduct themselves as adults. You can help break negative patterns in their lives and help train them up in the way they should go.

Some of you might be out there thinking, *It's great that your parents were fantastic role models for you and your siblings, but my parents weren't like that. I don't want to parent in the same way mine did.* If that's the case, you can make the decision to change that pattern and be a great role model for your kids. You don't have to perpetuate the cycle. I can tell you that you're already on the right path. The fact that you're reading books like this one means that you desire to make changes in your legacy. You can be a better parent than your own parents were.

Kids are watching, even when we think they're 100 percent focused on their video game. They are listening, even when they roll their adolescent eyes at us. They might not realize it, but we have a huge amount of influence over how they will turn out. Sure, they will make their own choices, which will include mistakes, but the way we train them up plays a great part in the decisions they will make in life.

CHAPTER 2

Whatever Happened to Predictability?

And Jesus increased in wisdom and in stature
and in favor with God and man.

—LUKE 2:52

• • • • • • • • • • • • •

The first time somebody watches a *Full House* episode, one of their first thoughts has to be: *How in the world did all of those people end up living together?* Well, it all happened because Pam Tanner (Danny's wife and the girls' mother) was killed in a car accident and Danny asked his brother-in-law Jesse and his best friend Joey to move in and help him raise the girls. One event— Pam's death—drastically changed the lives of six people in an instant.

We all experience various turning points or major events that cause huge changes in our lives. It probably just took you about two seconds to think about one of those moments in your own life. They're impossible to forget, because they shape us in big ways. Maybe you haven't experienced something as drastic as the Tanners did, but I'm sure each of you has had several experiences when one decision or one event—whether by your choice or not—radically altered nearly everything in your life.

I've discovered that sudden changes can easily lead to an imbalanced life and out-of-whack priorities if I'm not careful. I have had many of those turning points in my life, and you'll read about most of them throughout this book. I'll tell you the what, how, and why of these happenings or decisions, how my priorities shifted, and how I reestablished balance (or *didn't* reestablish balance) during those times.

For many people, most of those incidents happen during adulthood, but some of us deal with life-changing events in childhood. Unfortunately, many of these early experiences are unavoidable and can be unhappy occasions for the child: he or she becomes very sick, an immediate family member dies, parents get divorced, the family moves across the country and away from everything the child knows and loves, the child is removed from the home due to abuse or neglect, or a ton of other possible taxing situations. However, there are also instances when the major change is a happy time for the child and family as a whole, even though it might add an element of stress as well: a parent comes home from serving a military tour of duty, a new sibling is added to the family, a family in dire financial straits is suddenly relieved of that burden, or a child's parents get married. Granted, some of those events can also cause negative feelings in the child, but for the most part they're happy occurrences.

I think you can see where I'm going with this. I was one of those fortunate children who had a positive, life-changing event happen to me at a young age. The day I started working on *Full House*, my life changed forever. But I'm getting a little ahead of myself.

Balancing Entertainment

Oddly enough, my initial entrance into the entertainment industry at the age of five wasn't really a turning point for my family or me. It didn't really bring about any changes. Since two of my siblings had already been involved in the industry, adding one more didn't make a lot of difference. And I was young enough that I really didn't know any other lifestyle.

I enjoyed acting from the very beginning. In the early days, I never knew what a day would hold, but to a young kid that was exciting, not stressful. Commercial auditions took place after school hours, and Mom usually wouldn't find out about an audition until the actual day it happened. So every day I would walk out of the school building and look for Mom's car. If she was parked at the front of the line, I knew I had an audition. I'd hop into the car and prepare for the long ride. I always fell asleep and would be careful to keep my face from looking smashed in from the perforated dots on our fake leather seats. When we got there, I'd change into the clothes Mom had chosen for that particular audition, usually colorful overalls with high-top Converse sneakers. She also always brought along a butane-powered curling iron so she could quickly fix my hair before we rushed into the audition after our forty-five-minute drive into the heart of Los Angeles.

During those early years I did commercials for products and companies like Cabbage Patch Kids and Kentucky Fried Chicken. I also had a few small guest parts in some television series and TV movies. Eventually, I landed parts in the big-screen movies *Some Kind of Wonderful* and *Punchline*.

Around the time I auditioned for *Punchline* I also auditioned for *Full House*. I actually went through the first audition twice. After my first reading, the casting director told me she was going to call me back, but I also overheard her say on the phone to someone that I'd done "Okay," which was disappointing to me. Yes, I'd gotten the callback, but I knew I could be better than "okay." So Manager Mom convinced the casting director to give me another chance and tell me exactly what they wanted me to do. She knew that in auditions you aren't always given specific direction, but she also knew that if they gave me specific direction I would do exactly what I was told. She was right. My repeat audition was pronounced "great," much to my delight. I walked out of the room feeling much better about my prospects of getting the part. But before I got any official word about *Full House,* I was off to start filming *Punchline.*

I loved being on the *Punchline* set. It was filmed during the school year, so I was tutored on set, but I was happy to be there instead of playing with friends, because I really enjoyed my work. I was also very excited to be in a movie with Sally Field and Tom Hanks. I remember being so excited to work with Sally since my mom was such a huge fan. Sally was so caring, kind, and encouraging as a woman and an actress. I loved watching her and tried to take in everything I could as she performed her scenes.

As a ten-year-old, it was my job to know my lines and when to say them, but I didn't read the *Punchline* script in its entirety (because it wasn't totally appropriate for someone my age), so I really didn't know what kind of movie it was going to be or the feeling it was to portray. I just listened to the director tell me what to do. He gave me thoughts and emotions to think about and actions to do during the scene, and I would do it.

For the most part I watched in awe as Sally and John Goodman (who played my dad in the movie) did their thing. They were so invested, and only now can I look back and appreciate it. Talk about learning on the job; I was learning from the best! I also learned a lot more about the industry and figured out I needed to be very patient while on set. Since this was a big-budget film, each scene was filmed with a lot of care and time, which meant multiple takes, camera angles, and lens sizes. One scene could last a day. The next time you're in the movie theater watching the next big blockbuster, think about the fact that one two-minute scene likely took fourteen hours to film. To put that into perspective, my most recent two-hour TV movie was filmed in twelve days! But Sally taught me a great lesson during the *Punchline* filming. After about seven takes of a hysterical crying scene, she told the director she couldn't do any more. That stood out to me, because it taught me that even the best have their limits and it's okay to say when you've reached yours.

In the middle of filming *Punchline* we got the word that I had booked the part of *Full House*'s D.J. Tanner! However, we quickly learned that filming for the *Full House* pilot would conflict with my *Punchline* schedule, and I had an obligation to fulfill my movie contract. So Mom got my agent on the phone, and Iris made some calls to see what she could do. She found out that the *Full House* producers had liked me enough for the part that they would adjust the pilot filming schedule so I could be there. They had found their D.J. This is one of those everyday type examples of what it looks like to always understand and manage different priorities in your life. A key point to maintaining a healthy balance is being honest about too much on your plate or a conflict in schedules.

I was super excited about having booked the pilot. However, at the same time I knew the network had not yet picked up the show, so there were no guarantees. Mom and Dad both encouraged me to not get my hopes up too high. Many piloted shows never end up making it, and my parents didn't want me to be too upset if it didn't happen. I didn't know it at the time, but it was especially stressful for them since Kirk was already on a hit show. If my show wasn't picked up, they knew it would be a bigger deal for me than for many other kids simply because of the success of *Growing Pains*. It had to have been a huge balancing act for my parents to encourage me and be excited for the possibility while also helping to keep me grounded in the reality that my show might not make it. But . . . the network executives loved it, and I was finally able to be fully excited about the new direction my life was taking.

The Benefits of a Full House

Once we started filming the first season of *Full House*, the changes in my life were big and immediate. Since Kirk already had a lead part in a television show, my mom knew just what to expect. Thankfully, I had the benefit of seeing what Kirk's life was like, and Mom was able to help me navigate through the adjustments and keep all the various parts of my life going in a healthy manner. This is a good time to point out another key lesson about balancing it all—you can't do it alone. No one can. I'm thankful that my circumstances were such that I learned from a young age that having help knowing how to maintain balance as well as the help doing so is crucial. I definitely wouldn't have made it through the *Full House* season of my life without Mom's help with how to navigate all that was before me.

The biggest change during this new season of my life was that instead of just going to school every day, five days a week, I went to school *and* worked every day. We taped three weeks on, one week off, from July through April. Most people don't start putting in a full workweek until the age of eighteen or twenty-two, but I did it at ten . . . and I loved it!

The first year I was tutored on set. Jodie Sweetin (Stephanie Tanner), Andrea Barber (Kimmy Gibbler), and I would start school at 8:00 a.m. while the adults had rehearsal. We had to get in an average of three hours of school per day, but on Monday, Tuesday, and Wednesday, we would have four hours of school. This allowed us to "bank" three hours of school to apply toward Thursday and Friday, which were our taping days. So on those days we would only have an hour and a half of school. That gave us enough time to pretape our scenes and then tape the show in front of a live studio audience on Friday nights.

On Monday, Tuesday, and Wednesday, we would start rehearsal at 1:00 p.m. We would block our scenes, putting the show on its feet in its entirety. We did run-throughs at the end of the day on Tuesday and Wednesday for the writers, producers, and the network to watch. Then they would make more changes to the script in order to make it flow better or to get more laughs. From Monday through Wednesday I would leave the studio between 5:00 and 6:00 p.m.

During lunch on Wednesdays, we would have a read-through for the next week's episode. I loved this day, because it gave us a preview of what was to come and I always hoped the main story would be about D.J. Then on Thursday we pretaped the entire show so it was in the can in case we didn't get everything we needed in front of the live audience on Friday night. Because we had lots of little kids and dogs or other animals, this day always took the longest and we would work a full twelve hours.

On Fridays, we pulled into the studio around noon, finished up school, had a late lunch, and then got ready for our live audience show, which started at 5:00 p.m. It usually took four to five hours to tape, which meant half of our audience would leave before the show was over. For me, Friday nights were awesome, no matter how late they went. I loved getting laughs, and performing in front of people always upped everyone's game.

My new life was full and busy, but I loved every minute of it. Though it was hard work, it was also fun and exciting. It was so different from what I was used to, but I transitioned into this new world without a hitch.

Developing Balanced Lives

I fear I'm going to start sounding like a broken record in this area, but once again I believe that the reason for my smooth transition was due to my parents' influence in my life. The Bible says of parents, "When you walk, they will lead you; when you lie down, they will watch over you; and when you awake, they will talk with you" (Prov. 6:22). This perfectly describes the way my parents guided me as a child.

When I was ten years old, there is no way I would have been able to balance and prioritize my new life on my own, so I am extremely grateful for my parents' wisdom and guidance during that time. My parents knew what was important for me. They knew the ways in which they needed to care for me, and they understood the areas where I needed to grow.

Children typically don't have as many things to balance in their lives as adults do, but they do need to grow in a balanced way. We don't read much in the Bible about the lives of children, and it contains only twelve verses about Jesus' childhood, but the final one says all we really need to know about how a child should grow. "And Jesus increased in wisdom and in stature and in favor with God and man" (Luke 2:52). What does this mean for us? To have balanced lives, we are to grow in four ways: intellectually, physically, spiritually, and socially.

My parents—especially my teacher father—placed a high importance on education. Rest assured that my parents wanted me to not only learn academically, but they also taught me how to make wise and practical choices in all areas of my life. Physically, Mom and Dad made sure I took care of my body by feeding me, clothing me, and keeping me safe. As for my spiritual growth, even though my dad didn't realize he was teaching me biblical principles for living, he did it. Yes, my parents could have nurtured my spiritual life from an earlier age than they did, but I am grateful that we eventually started going to church so that I could begin to have a relationship with God. Finally, my social growth—relationships with others—was always in bloom. My parents placed a high value on family and on friendships. They made sure I had plenty of healthy interaction with others so I could grow into a socially adept young woman.

Even though I had a drastic life change at a young age and my childhood was vastly different from that of most other children, the principles behind creating a balanced life were the same as if I had experienced a "normal" childhood, and I believe they would have been the same if I had been born into an impoverished family on the other side of the world. No matter who we are or what our circumstances are, there are basic areas of life that we need to balance both as children and as adults.

Being honest about when you have too much on your plate or a conflict in schedules is a crucial way that we maintain balance. You may not be juggling a film roll and a new television show like I was, but I bet you have times when you are supposed to be in two places at once or maybe your kids have soccer practice at the same time as debate club. Or, if you are me, your boys have hockey games in separate arenas at the same time. In these instances we must confront the conflict directly, acknowledge that we cannot do it all, and be comfortable with not always being able to do it all.

We need to also remember that we can't do it all on our own. This was true for me as a child, but not only because I was a child. It was because we always need the help of others and that is especially true when we are launching into a new season of life. It is important to have people in your life who share your values, are honest, and will be there for you—just as you are for them!

Finally, we need to keep in mind our role to pour into the lives of those around us—certainly our children, but also our friends, other family members, and those closest to us. Growing and maintaining a healthy balance in our lives is key to that. As I said earlier, we need to ensure we are growing intellectually, physically, spiritually, and socially. We've probably all met someone who is very well developed in one of these areas and underdeveloped in another. As you read and think about what it will mean to balance it all in your life, think about how your priorities can help you grow in each of these ways to be all that God has designed you to be!

CHAPTER 3

A Heart Change

I will give you a new heart and put a new spirit
within you; I will remove your heart of stone
and give you a heart of flesh.
—Ezekiel 36:26 (hcsb)

• • • • • • • • • • • •

If you watched *Make It or Break It* there is probably one main character that made you mad more times than anyone else: Lauren Tanner. Lauren was often vicious, vindictive, and just flat-out mean to the other gymnasts (including her best friends), the coaches, her parents, and basically anyone else with whom she came into contact. By all accounts, she had a heart of stone. My character, Summer van Horne, dated Lauren's dad during the first season and became a kind of surrogate mother to Lauren.

Summer shared her Christian faith and the principles she knew were effective in her life, and she tried to help Lauren become a better person—a person with a heart of flesh. While Lauren did eventually start treating people a little better thanks to Summer's influence, viewers always questioned her motives. Why? Because she still often treated people badly and there wasn't a lot of evidence that Lauren had changed on the inside. When it comes down to it, you can't really change on the outside until you change on the inside.

So how does this relate to balance and priorities? Well, I've found that many times my life is out of balance and my priorities need to change because *I* need to change. The things I do are based on the state of my heart at that time. My heart needs to change so that I can see clearly to make wise choices about how I live my life.

My life often gets thrown out of balance when I start considering what is acceptable to the world—our culture, the media, Hollywood, etc.—instead of what is acceptable to God. Romans 12:2 says, "Do not be conformed to this world, but be transformed by the renewal of your mind, that by testing you may discern what is the will of God, what is good and acceptable and perfect." When I get caught up in what the world deems important, my mind needs to be renewed—something inside me needs to change—in order for me to see and do what God wants for me. When I start to get selfish, focused on material things, or put too much of a focus on work over my family, I need to make an adjustment. Yes, my actions and decisions need to change, but in order for that to happen, my heart needs to change. I need to see my part in the problem and ask God to transform me from the inside so that I can be in His good, acceptable, and perfect will.

I wasn't always aware of this concept, nor did I look to God when I knew I needed to make adjustments in my life. But I started to get a glimpse of it when my parents separated for a time. You thought my family was perfect? Sorry to disappoint you, but we had our share of problems too.

Family Heartbreak

Mom and Dad were always focused on what was best for us kids. You moms out there might be wondering how they did it all with Kirk and me both working on different TV shows every day. Well, thankfully Kirk turned sixteen soon after *Full House* began, so he was able to drive himself to and from work. That freed Mom up to take me where I needed to be. However, she had two daughters at home, was managing both Kirk and me, and still needed to be involved in the day-to-day details of Kirk's career, so she would often go back and forth between home and the two sets, and she would leave me under the watchful care and guardianship of our studio teacher when she wasn't able to be on the *Full House* set.

Meanwhile, Dad was still being Mr. Mom at home with Bridgette and Melissa while Mom was with Kirk and me. Once I started working full-time I missed spending the afternoons with my sisters. On some days I was a little jealous that they were getting to play and hang out and have fun together while I was working. But overall, I was extremely excited and happy to be on the show, and it really helped that I loved my *Full House* family. They weren't quite as great as the Cameron family, but they were right up there!

Even with all the craziness going on with two kids on two different TV shows, my parents continued to insist on keeping family time a priority, keeping us as grounded as possible, and setting reasonable boundaries for us. Mom and Dad did not want us kids involved in the Hollywood lifestyle. Other teen stars were often featured in the tabloids for various indiscretions, and my parents had no intention of letting us be a part of the party crowd and messing up our lives, careers, and futures. Even though Kirk and I were making much more money than our parents made, they made sure we stayed respectful, realized we were no better than our sisters, and knew who the parents were. All four of us had rules just like any typical teenagers: chores, curfews, dating age, when we could wear makeup, and even when we could start shaving our legs! We didn't get a different set of rules just because two of us were on TV.

We were taught to treat others with respect, and that meant on the set as well as off it. We were to respect all of the crew on the set, whether they were the producers or the janitors. Also, after a tape day, Mom expected me to hang up my clothes. This was unexpected by the wardrobe people; apparently not everyone bothered to hang their clothes back up. But to me, it was just normal, as was cleaning up my dressing room each day. I had chores at home, and I had chores at work.

While my parents seemed to have it all together when it came to parenting, that was not so much the case with their marriage. I could tell they were often frustrated with each other. Several times a week they would have closed-door meetings in their bedroom, and I knew it wasn't for anything fun. They were constantly talking through things, being very specific in the way they worded their sentences with one another. They met with friends for counsel several nights a week.

One night Mom was very upset and in tears. She asked me to pack my overnight bag because we were going to spend the night at an inn down the street. Several hours after we arrived at the hotel, Dad knocked on the door. When Mom opened it, he was crying and pleading to talk with her. As a twelve-year-old I couldn't figure out which one of them had done something bad. Who was to blame for whatever the problem was? Based on the desperate looks on both of their faces that night, I couldn't come to a conclusion.

I knew things weren't good, but it did seem as if they were working on things, so it came as a shock when my mom said she was moving out of the house. Thankfully, the possibility of divorce never really entered my mind. I figured Mom and Dad needed a break, but they would work it out.

So Mom got an apartment close to home and I spent much of my time there, since she was the one who drove me to and from work. I have to admit that it was kind of fun to shop for new furniture, linens, and kitchen items for the apartment. It seemed more like a vacation rental than my mom's new permanent residence. When I really thought about it, though, I felt like it was a joke that had been taken too far. The apartment didn't feel like home, and some days I was really sad and just wanted to go back to my real house. I wanted everyone to return to our normal family life.

A Surprise Outing

One evening when I was staying at "Dad's house," he told my sisters and me to jump in the car, but he wouldn't tell us where we were going. It was quite a surprise when we pulled up to a big warehouse-type building and discovered Dad had brought us to church. We sat in the back row with Dad's friend who had invited us. It was weird being there, but at the same time I knew it was a huge deal because my dad was the last person I ever thought would go to church. This was the man who didn't want Mom taking us to church, yet here we were! But even at that young age I realized that this was Dad's way of trying to make changes in his heart and attitude. He was seeking help to revive his marriage. That was a major moment in my life—seeing my dad do something so humble for the sake of his wife and kids.

We started going to church every Sunday, and the more I went the more I liked it. At first I would just go to the service in the main sanctuary, but then I found out about the middle school Sunday school class I could attend with other kids my age. I went a few times, but I didn't really feel like I fit in because I was so new to anything that had to do with church and the Bible. All of the other kids knew so much more than I did. We would share with each other in small groups, but I mostly sat there quietly listening. I really had no clue what they were talking about, and I didn't know any of the people in the Bible or their historical accounts. I realized I liked sitting in the main sanctuary and listening to the sermons, even though it sounded so foreign. I preferred to get an overview of what the pastor was talking about instead of trying to figure out the specifics of the Bible at that time.

After we began attending church, I really started to see some changes in my dad. He had always been a good and generous person, but he previously had a negative spirit and wasn't always encouraging. But he started to change in those areas, and I think Mom saw that. Not long after, Mom said she was coming home. I was so thrilled! I had always felt in my heart that it would happen and I never gave up hope that she would return.

Mom was going to church with us, and it made me so happy to see her smiling when she was there. The people at that church seemed so kind, loving, and friendly, and my family greatly benefited from that. But more than that, we profited from the change God was bringing about in both of my parents. Dad had certainly started doing everything he could to be the kind of man my mom and us kids needed him to be. It was obvious that those changes weren't just superficial—he was truly changing on the inside. I don't believe that would have been possible without God's help.

Spiritual Adjustments

Meanwhile, I enjoyed going to church every week and getting to know a whole new group of people that seemed positive and optimistic—and who loved God. It was only months before I decided to give my heart to Jesus. At the end of one church service, I repeated the pastor's prayer and then raised my hand to show that I had asked Jesus to be my Savior. At twelve years old, I believed He had died to pay for my sins and saved me from an eternity in hell. A few weeks later, my mom, brother, sister, cousin, and I were all baptized. Dad wasn't baptized at the time, but it was obvious God was working in him.

If you've been around church much, you know that most churches have a youth group, and ours was no exception. I went quite a bit during the summer, but it was hard during the months I was working on the show. However, when I was fourteen I was excited to get to go on my first youth group weekend retreat to Big Bear, California. The rest of the kids went up to the retreat site on the church bus on Friday, but it was during taping season for *Full House,* and we had our live tapings on Fridays. I was so excited about my first retreat, though, that my parents agreed to make the three-hour drive early Saturday morning so I could join my friends at Big Bear. Unfortunately, I got so sick that

Saturday afternoon that I wanted to go home immediately. I couldn't endure the thought of being there another day and then riding the bus back home on Monday when all I could think about was throwing up. So Mom and Dad drove back up to Big Bear early Sunday morning to pick me up. Even though my first "camp" experience didn't turn out like I'd hoped it would, it showed me how much my parents loved me and how far they were willing to go to help make my life as normal as possible during my teen years.

After a while, Kirk started going to a new church and I joined him. It was much smaller than our previous church, and it didn't have a youth group, but I had a crush on one of my brother's friends so I was more than happy to go. Yeah, I know I'm not the only teen who went to church because of a member of the opposite sex! Whoever God uses, right?

We continued to go to church as a family, but as I got into my mid-teen years, church got put on the back burner. I was traveling a lot on the weekends and I was exhausted. Even when we were home on Sundays Mom and Dad didn't always make me go to church, though they typically went and let me sleep in. Other than my dad's transformation of attitude and behavior, our home life didn't change a whole lot because of church. We were still morally guided in a biblical way, but we didn't read the Bible as a family or pray together. Honestly, we didn't talk about God much. We all kind of did our own thing. I saw Mom read the Bible a lot, and Dad read a lot of books about the Bible because he was still trying to grasp his understanding of God from a scientific background, but other than going to the occasional Sunday morning service, my life wasn't much different than before.

A New Beginning

My dad's life was different, however, and that affected the whole family in a positive way. I don't think it's a coincidence that Dad started to change at the same time we started going to church. When we want God to change us, He will. When we follow Him, He will transform us. Second Corinthians 5:17 says, "Therefore, if anyone is in Christ, he is a new creation. The old has passed away; behold, the new has come." God makes us new.

I believe God made my parents' marriage new. They were very committed to each other, and they put a lot of time and effort into their marriage. They both desperately wanted to make it work, so much that they were both willing to change what needed to be changed. My dad became a different man before our eyes, and my mom became more confident. When things got to a point where they knew they had to change, they sought out God, and He gave them the strength to do it.

My parents' marriage—through the good times and the bad times—has made a huge impact on my life both when I was a kid and today. I saw the struggle, I saw them take the steps they needed to take to change and make it work, and I saw them never give up. I believe this illustrates that when you put in the time and effort and strive to follow God, He will bless your actions when they fall in line with His will.

Mom and Dad's story gives me an amazing amount of hope when it comes to my own marriage. There's just no way I could quit, even in an especially hard season of marriage, because I've seen firsthand what God can do when both parties have open hearts and are willing to change.

Changes of Heart

That principle plays out in all parts of life. When we know something is off track in our lives, typically something inside us needs to change in order to get back on the right path. If your life is out of balance right now and your priorities aren't right, consider how you might need to change on the inside. Maybe your sense of identity is tied to your job or your boyfriend. Maybe it's all about being a mom. There are definitely seasons in our life when we need to focus on a particular area of our lives, but we end up in trouble when our identity is tied to what is just supposed to be a priority. Life will definitely end up out of balance. At that point, we need to step back and consider what changes we need to make. But it's not just about changing our choices related to balance, it's about changing the way we view ourselves and our lives so that balance flows out of a right heart.

Just as the changes I saw in my family helped lead me to evaluating my own heart for change, the example of our lives is hugely significant to those around us. We learn from those around us—both the good and the bad. And I believe there is no better person to model your life after than Jesus Christ. So as my husband and I work to keep our marriage strong, guide and lead our children, and make wise decisions, my desire is for us to grow just like Jesus did and to be imitators and followers of Christ. It's the example of Jesus who balanced mercy and justice, humility and strength—and ultimately being both God and man. To the degree that my life has had any balance it is all because of principles that tie back to Him!

CHAPTER 4

You've Got a Friend in Me

Two are better than one because they have a good reward
for their efforts. For if either falls, his companion can lift him
up; but pity the one who falls without another to lift him up.
—ECCLESIASTES 4:9–10 (HCSB)

• • • • • • • • • • • • • •

I f you're a blogger, you know the scenario all too well. You post your article and if there's something for someone to challenge, the comments come streaming in. That was the case with an interview I gave that was published on a very popular magazine's website. They had asked me about baby advice and what my go-to recommendation was for a first-time mom. I casually answered with the title of a book that I used to help me get all three of my kids sleeping through the night and on an eating, sleeping, and playing schedule by twelve weeks old.

Little did I know that in some mom circles the book wasn't very popular, and I had more than my fair share of hate comments pouring in. I didn't even know the article had been posted until my best friend Dilini called me. She was audibly upset and told me she had my back. She was outraged over the attacks. True to best friend form, Dilini commented alongside everyone else, defending my statement, my character as a mom, and my choice of parenting style, even though she didn't have kids, because she's seen it work firsthand with me and with several other mom friends. You have to love your BFF standing up for you, even when you don't even know you need it!

The verse from Ecclesiastes at the beginning of this chapter beautifully sums up one of the greatest reasons friendships are important. We enjoy friends during the good times, but we *need* them during the bad times. When you read that verse, which of your friends came to mind? I'm sure somebody did—whether it's somebody who is currently in your life or someone from the past that you wish was still in your life.

We all know that friendships take work, especially at the beginning. Like most things, we get out of relationships what we put into them. If we don't invest a lot of time into a friendship, it either won't last or it won't be satisfying. Sometimes life gets hectic with family, work, church, volunteering, and a million other things, and we're tempted to put our pals on the back burner. But without relationships with other women, I don't think our lives can be truly balanced. God created us for connection with others, and not just with our families. Friends can give us a different perspective on life, can see things in us that family members may be too close to see, and can often get away with saying things to us that spouses, kids, or parents can't. I will admit that siblings might be an exception to that last statement, which is why they make some of the best friends!

I don't know what I would do without Dilini, my best friend of more than twenty years. We talk every few days, if not more often. If there's exciting news, she's the first person to hear it, and vice versa. If I'm upset, Dilini's who I call. She is always there for me and has lifted me up more times than I can count. If you don't have an ally and supporter like Dilini, I pray that you'll find one soon.

School Days, School Days

I met Dilini at school when we were in tenth grade. Wait a minute . . . wasn't I tutored on set? I was, with a few exceptions.

When I was in junior high, I decided to go to public school for two hours in the morning in order to try to create a little bit of normalcy in my life. Then I'd head to the set and do a couple of hours of tutoring until it was time to get to work in the afternoon. However, instead of creating normalcy, that setup created a ripe environment for bullying. You know how it can be in junior high. Kids are brutal, and they didn't give me a break because of my TV-star status. In fact, that just made it worse. I was picked on all the time. My one saving grace during those years was my best friend Alli, who I met in seventh grade. We had slumber parties too numerous to count, and in the summertime we'd lay out by her pool and prank call boys. Once we were old enough to drive, we spent most of our time at the mall shopping and eating sushi.

By the time ninth grade came around, I couldn't take public school anymore because of the teasing, so I was tutored on set again. Even though I didn't miss actually going to school, I did miss hanging out with my friends. I recall one night when Mom and I were driving home from work. I hadn't hung out with friends in what felt like months. I didn't get home until 7:00 or 8:00 every night, and Friday night tapings usually lasted until 11:00 p.m. It was hard to find time to spend with friends. I just wanted to go to a movie. To my surprise, Mom was really supportive even though it was a work night for me and a school night for everyone else. She let me call as many friends as I could to see if anyone was able to go out with me. Unfortunately, none of them were, but knowing my mom understood and tried to help me make it happen is a memory that has stuck with me to this day.

It was a pivotal moment for me when I realized that Mom was on my side and understood that "normal" was not in my future. I appreciated her willingness to go against our traditional household rules for once and allow me to try to spend some much-needed time with friends, even though it didn't work out.

For tenth grade, my parents and I decided I would try integrating my on-set tutoring studies with a private school. Because it was so small and the students were few, it was a much better fit for me than public school had been. The kids were great and I made several lifelong friends. The only drawback was that since it was a college prep school, it ended up being too much of a challenge for me to handle along with a full-time job.

I remember one time during tenth grade when I was called into the dean's office. I had been skipping first hour homeroom one day a week because I was tired in the mornings and didn't see the importance of sitting in the classroom with nothing to do. It was really for attendance, and not much else was accomplished during that time. I had plenty of other things I could be doing instead, like sleeping, catching up on homework, or learning lines. When I was honest with the dean about why I'd been skipping that class with my parents' approval, he was concerned by my attitude; it seemed as if school wasn't a priority to me. I took a deep breath and boldly told him as respectfully as I could that getting into an Ivy League college was of no concern to me. My job was my main focus at that time in my life. I explained that I could be tutored on the set but had decided to go to school simply to have friends and a sense of normalcy along with a good education. But I was not there to compete for a coveted spot at an excellent university. He was dumbfounded, and for good reason! He had never encountered a teenager who had a full-time job! Due to my atypical lifestyle, my priorities were quite different than those of nearly every other high schooler he had ever known.

Halfway through my eleventh grade year, I convinced my parents to allow me to be tutored full-time on set once again. But even though my time at Viewpoint School was challenging, it gave me one thing that tutoring on the set of *Full House* couldn't have given me: Dilini.

The Beginning of a Beautiful Friendship

When I started at Viewpoint, it was a bit awkward because most of the other kids had attended the school since kindergarten. They all knew each other, and I was the new kid on the block. Dilini was the student in charge of greeting the "newbies," which is how we first connected. Viewpoint was very small at the time—about thirty kids in each grade—and at the end of the summer each class would have a party so the students could reconnect before school started. Dilini got the class list so she could invite everyone and she discovered that her new classmate was Candace Cameron from *Full House*. Needless to say, she was very nervous about calling me because, well, I was on TV. (Who knew I could be so intimidating?) We chatted for a few minutes, and she was really sweet, but it turned out that I wouldn't be able to attend the party because of work.

I did meet Dilini once school started, because we had classes together, but it wasn't until a couple of months later that we began hanging out. We discovered that we lived less than two miles from each other, so one night we decided to study together. From that moment on we were fast friends.

Dilini's parents were a lot like mine: strict and protective. They had a rule that they wouldn't let her hang out with a new person until they had met the friend and her parents.

I learned they were even more skeptical of me because I was in show business. I honestly don't blame them, considering the culture in which most Hollywood kids are immersed. But they hadn't yet met my parents. When Dilini's dad came over to meet my dad, he realized he had met his match! The two of them completely hit it off and chatted for an hour that first night. Over time, our families became very close, and we celebrate Thanksgiving and New Year's Day together every year to this day.

Once I left Viewpoint, I made a point to keep my friendship with Dilini a priority. If I was on location for a summer job I would fly her in so we could spend several days together. When we were seventeen, I was asked to be the Grand Marshal of the 4th of July Parade and festivities in San Diego. It was a three-hour drive from L.A., with events that would require a two-night stay. My parents talked with Alli's and Dilini's parents and decided that we were mature enough that they would allow us to go on the trip without them as chaperones. Talk about girl time! We still reminisce about all the fun we had on that trip, like singing our guts out to SWV and Boyz II Men on the limo ride home. I have that on video somewhere, but I promise I'll never share!

During the last year of *Full House*, after we had graduated from high school, I'd go hang out with Dilini and her friends at college, or she'd come have lunch with me on the set. Even though we were still fairly young, we did whatever we needed to do in order to foster and maintain our friendship, even though our life paths were very different.

Fax Machines and Spice Girls

On August 18, 1994, Dilini moved into her dorm room at the University of Southern California, and I was right there with her parents and sister helping her unload, unpack her clothes, and meet her new roomies. That evening I had plans to go to a charity hockey game with Dave Coulier, who had a certain player he wanted me to meet. Dilini invited me to stay at USC and experience her first night of college life with her, but I chose to go with Dave, and am I ever glad, because that's the night I met Val!

After I saw Val the second time (a few months after our initial meeting . . . you'll hear more about that later!), I immediately called Dilini. You younger readers probably don't think that's a big deal, since your cell phone has been your constant companion since middle school, if not before. But anyone who grew up in the technological stone age like I did will understand that I had to go out of my way to make that call back in 1994. I had to use an actual pay phone at the airport in Fredericton, New Brunswick. And you will laugh at the fact that I sent her a FAX from Paris to announce my engagement!

Dilini was with me when Lev was born. I had decided to deliver in the U.S., so I had gone back to Los Angeles for several weeks. Dilini slept over at my house the night before I was scheduled to be induced because Val was still playing in Calgary. He flew in that morning and met us at the hospital, but at 4:30 a.m. my best friend drove me to the hospital and stayed by my side. She missed Maks's birth because we were living in Florida, but I called her as soon as he entered the world. What about Natasha's birth? Well (hold your technological snickering), I *paged* Dilini the morning I went into labor so she would know to head to the hospital. However, she didn't receive the page until twelve hours later, after Natasha had already been born. Where was Dilini when the page finally came through? She was at a Spice Girls concert! It's become the perpetual joke and Natasha never fails to remind Dilini that she missed her birth for a little zig-a-zig-ah.

The two of us have always spent time together whenever we can, even when we've lived in different countries. We've always made it a point to fly to see each other on our birthdays and any time either of us was able to make an extra trip just to hang out, we would. And now that we're both back in L.A., she's my wing-girl for all Hollywood parties and events since Val isn't into people-watching and celebrity-sighting nearly as much as we are! Talk about two giddy thirty-some-thing-year-olds; you'd think we were at a NKOTB concert all the time!

Dilini is also happy to be a third wheel at times when it's just me and Val, and I'm so thankful that the two of them love each other and get along so well. She spends a lot of time with my whole family, and she is faithful to attend my kids' birthday parties, hockey games, plays, and anything else that is important to us. Dilini is a familiar face to anyone in my circles and everyone just kind of expects her to be where my family is, and I love that. For me, the best part about her is the listening ear she provides when this girl just needs to vent. She is truly like a sister to me.

Differences Make the World Go 'Round

When it comes to friendships, it's a must to have things in common, but I think your differences are just as impor-tant. Dilini and I love and appreciate each other for both our similarities and our differences. When friends can comple-ment each other and challenge each other, that gives both people a chance to grow.

One way that Dilini and I complement each other is through our personalities. In new environments or situa-tions, she's more outgoing and I'm more introverted, although

I've come a long way. If we're at a party, she wants to interact with people and get into conversations, but I tend to clam up. So she'll challenge me to be bold and chat with people instead of just sitting in a corner. I could people-watch all night, but at the end of the evening, that's not nearly as satisfying as meeting new people, having great conversations, and getting an occasional picture with someone I admire.

I think you'd probably agree with me that honesty is perhaps the single most important factor in any relationship. Dilini and I are always 100 percent honest with each other, and I think that's the biggest reason why our friendship works. In twenty-two years we've never had a fight with each other, and I chalk that up to honesty. We consider each other's feelings, and if at times either of us is unintentionally insensitive, we immediately call it out and work through it. Nothing festers, and bitterness isn't allowed to sneak in. You've probably heard the saying, "Do not let the sun go down on your anger." (Did you know it comes from the Bible? You can find it in Ephesians 4:26.) Many people only apply that rule to their spouse, but I think it's a great principle to live by when it comes to anyone—including friends. In fact, I think a lot of anger can actually be avoided if we just talk through things before they get to that point.

Many of you will be surprised to know that Dilini and I do not share the same faith or political convictions. I am a conservative evangelical Christian, and she is a Buddhist and conservative liberal. We respect each other's differences and don't try to argue, debate, or persuade each other to our views and beliefs in a demeaning or disgruntled way. We share and discuss respectfully. As we both evolve as people in life, faith, and circumstances, we keep sharing and discussing even if we know we won't see eye to eye on everything. I don't stop talking to her about my faith and love for Jesus just because she doesn't put her faith in Him, but I also don't shove my views down her throat, nor does she do that to me.

Please understand that I do think it is important to have friends that share my faith, and I have plenty of those. But I think we also need to be friends with people who think differently than we do. It gives us a bigger view of the world, it helps us to understand different sides of an issue, and it also gives us opportunities to really figure out what we believe. After all, Proverbs 27:17 says, "Iron sharpens iron, and one man sharpens another." We would never grow if we didn't have anyone to challenge us. When we have strong friendships with people that we disagree with on some of the big issues in life, we can't ignore those issues. It forces us to put words (and ultimately actions) to our beliefs. And when it comes down to it, if we were to only be friends with people who hold the exact same beliefs or opinions as we do on everything, none of us would have any friends.

True Friends

Dilini is and always has been a true friend to me. People have different opinions about what makes a true friend, but I think the Bible says it best. Proverbs 17:17 says, "A friend loves at all times." True friends accept you unconditionally. They stick by you through thick and thin and don't give up on you when the going gets rough. "Greater love has no one than this, that someone lay down his life for his friends" (John 15:13). A true friend's love is sacrificial; she is unselfish and considers what she can do for you.

If you have one or more true friends that accept you unconditionally, sacrificially, and unselfishly, and are there to lift you up when you fall, I am thrilled for you! But I'm guessing some of you may not have that kind of friend right now. Sometimes the craziness of life gets in the way and friendships have fallen by the wayside, or circumstances like a recent move or divorce haven't allowed you to find the confidant you're looking for. It's not uncommon for women to have phases in life when we don't have many, if any, close friends. If that's you, I want to encourage you to do whatever it takes to make friendships a priority. Pray that God will provide some true friends, and then put yourself out there.

Over the years, Dilini and many other friends have been great encouragers and have lifted me up when I've fallen. I can't count the times that one of them has been there for me when I've needed her. If there ever was a time I needed a friend but didn't get the help I wanted, it's simply because I didn't ask for it. It's comforting to have a few special friends in life that you know will always be there for you.

Balancing Friendship

As you think about what it looks like to maintain balance in your life, I want to encourage you to evaluate your friendships. Do you have at least one good friend who you can trust? Do you have friends who share your faith and values? Do you also have friends who help you to understand and respect other viewpoints? These are all areas of balance that you can see I've gotten through friendship. I've focused here on my friendship with Dilini, as she's my best friend and she is instrumental in helping me stay balanced. But if you read my book *Reshaping It All,* you probably remember me talking about my friend Mandy and her family. They are also great friends and contribute a lot to my ability to balance my life.

I have found that friendships are not only crucial to balance, they are one of the most natural ways we find balance. Once you take the intentional step to make time for friendships in the midst of everything else you are balancing, you will discover that the sounding board of a good friend is a great benefit to helping balance the opportunities, priorities, and challenges of life. In fact, this represents one of the key lessons about balance I've learned in my life—although it takes time to invest in relationships, healthy relationships contribute to your life in such a way that you can do *more* with them than you could without them! This is true of marriage, parenting, friendships, and certainly a relationship with God.

As you read about my relationship with Dilini, you may have thought of your best friend. If this is true for you, let me encourage you to write a quick text or e-mail (thankfully, you don't have to fax!) to your best friend and thank her for all the ways she helps balance out your life. Or maybe you struggled through this chapter because you realized that you don't have a friendship like this, but really want one. Perhaps you can think of an acquaintance or old friend with whom you would like to spend more time. All friendships take someone stepping out to strengthen the relationship. Reach out and invite the person who comes to mind to coffee or over for dinner. I hope that this small step will lead to a friendship as strong and long as mine with Dilini—remember, ours started with a brief phone call and look where we are decades later!

CHAPTER 5

Are We Having Fun Yet?

A joyful heart is good medicine,
but a crushed spirit dries up the bones.
—Proverbs 17:22

• • • • • • • • • • • • • •

You know how they say that work doesn't feel like work if you're passionate about it? That's how I feel about making movies and television. I love acting so much and I'm in one of my happiest places when I'm on set. I recently filmed an Up Network movie called *Finding Normal* in Columbia, Louisiana, and I had an absolute blast. Not only was the atmosphere on set lighthearted despite the unfortunate weather, but I don't know that I can recall more impromptu Bon Jovi songs, Carlton Banks-style dance moves, and flat-out corny jokes while making a movie.

I laughed so hard that I howled through tears, hunched over and holding my stomach because it hurt so much. If you didn't know already, I'm a self-proclaimed goofball and "silly" is my middle name. I'm not gonna lie, there was karaoke each Friday night and I sang my heart out to every *Grease* song on the soundtrack. Please, if you were there or have videos, I don't want to see them!

Since I routinely have a great time both at work and at home, it amazes me that so many people often forget to keep fun on their list of priorities. Think for a minute about the last time you broke out in laughter. Was it sometime today, or was it a long time ago? If you don't instinctively have fun throughout your life, I want to encourage you to start planning your own entertainment by doing things and being around people that make you happy. Eventually you won't have to plan it anymore. It will just happen!

We must remember to find merriment on a regular basis, whether it's a planned event or just playing a spontaneous game with your kids. When we have fun, it puts us in a better mood, we smile, and typically we become more positive about things. And, for a while, we might even forget about the hardships in our lives and simply enjoy living. Take a look at the word *enjoy* for a moment. What's the word within that word? Joy! Proverbs 17:22 says that "a joyful heart is good medicine." I agree. When we enjoy life, it changes our hearts and our lives. It simply makes us feel better.

Of course, there are times and seasons in life when some people tend to put too much of an emphasis on having a good time, at the expense of something more important. Anyone reading this who has failed a class because of having too much "fun" on nights and weekends knows exactly what I'm talking about. (Your parents do too!) Or maybe you've fallen behind on work obligations because sometimes staying out late with your girlfriends just feels like a better idea. It's definitely possible to get sidetracked and neglect your family, job, education, or other priorities due to focusing too much on having a good time. But for the most part, adults—especially busy moms—tend to live dull, boring lives because we're so worried about sticking to the schedule and checking off everything on our to-do list each day. We can quickly get overwhelmed and feel weighed down.

I realize that in the craziness of life sometimes it seems making room for joy should be the first thing to go when you simply don't have enough time for everything. But when you consider that you can actually have fun while doing the other "important" things, it brings a different perspective. Sneak some amusement into family meal times by playing a board game during dessert or use a crazy accent or a goofy voice when you read books to your kids. (As a side note, embarrassing my teens gives me great joy and the best laughs. How many times have I heard Natasha say to me, "Mom! You *cannot* say the words *cray cray*. It's just *wrong!*") And if you don't have kids, schedule that dinner date with your hubby and enjoy some alone time. Bring in an unexpected treat for your coworkers and enjoy the smiles. Call your best friend and go for a bike ride. Involve as many people in your fun as you can. They'll more than likely thank you for it.

Having a Blast

During my *Full House* days I greatly benefited from other people bringing fun into my life. Working forty-plus hours a week is definitely not a typical lifestyle for a teenager, so I'm glad the people around me made sure I enjoyed myself while I was on the job.

In addition to rehearsing and taping the show, I did a lot of public appearances on weekends, which was often a tiring experience due to the logistics and long days. I enjoyed meeting fans and signing autographs. It was cool to hear their stories and see their smiles when they saw or met me.

For the most part, my appearances went smoothly, but there were a few that didn't. There was one signing I will never forget. A mall in Canada had prepared for between 3,000 and 5,000 people to show up to see me. Instead, nearly

20,000 fans came. Cars were parked everywhere, including along the highway exit ramps. Due to the miscalculation of numbers, there weren't enough security officers on duty. It was a madhouse and there was no way I could have signed autographs for that many people. It simply wasn't physically possible. Even worse, they didn't have the manpower or preparation to corral that many people in an orderly and smooth fashion. I stayed a few hours after the official ending time of the signing to get to as many people as possible, but eventually security simply had to get me out of there in order to control the chaos. Disappointing so many people made my heart sink.

Though he couldn't control everything, my manager Jonathan (Mom had moved on to agenting by then) was brilliant when it came to making public appearances enjoyable for me. He would come up with a theme for the year, so I would have something to look forward to in each city. He was a huge Cleveland Browns fan, and I jumped on the bandwagon, so one year we scheduled my entire appearance schedule based on where the Browns were playing. I would do my appearance on a Saturday, and then we'd watch the game on Sunday. I'm still a Browns fan to this day because of that. (Go Dawgs! Woof!) Another year we scheduled my appearances in cities that had theme parks. Our goal was to determine which one had the best roller coasters.

Whenever it was possible schedule-wise, Mom would make sure our whole family could go on work trips with me. We would typically receive two first-class plane tickets for on-location shoots—one for me and one for Mom. But we knew it would be more fun if we all went, so Mom would exchange those tickets for a handful of economy tickets so my dad and sisters could come along to make it more enjoyable for all of us. Remember those Hawaii episodes on *Full House* and *Growing Pains?* My whole family was there. We were all in Orlando, too, for the Disney World episodes!

In addition to my parents and my manager, I had three other adults in my life who made sure I enjoyed my job. Bob Saget, Dave Coulier, and John Stamos definitely ensured everyone had a great time on the set. If you remember D.J.'s date with some guy in a van, you'll love hearing the back-story to that pre-tape night. For reasons I don't recall, the night had gotten late, my legal working hours were almost up, and we were in a rush to finish up. D.J. was supposed to be "making out" with her date in his van, and Danny, Jesse, and Joey were supposed to spy on them, catch them kissing (or worse), and rescue their little girl. Giddiness set in and the guys couldn't keep it together. They'd walk around the corner of the van, starting out with concerned expressions, only to bust into laughter halfway through their lines. This went on for what seemed like forever! Take one, take ten, take twenty-five! The producers and director were tired and pleaded with the guys to get in one good and usable take. They agreed to get it together. However, the next time they rounded the corner of the van, they had their tuxedo pants down around their ankles, boxer shorts showing under their white button-down shirts and jackets, looking like penguins! We all just roared. It was absolutely hysterical and I'll never forget it.

One time we were all goofing off so much—mostly the guys, really—that the director Joel Zwick got really upset and called for an immediate meeting with the cast to have a stern talk with us. But when we all met in the green room, what he wasn't expecting were four little angelic faces (me, Jodie, Mary Kate, and Ashley) looking up at him among the guys. He couldn't quite yell at us the way he intended to with just the guys, and he basically melted. So thanks to us girls, we ended up hearing only a very moderate speech about getting the job done and pulling it together.

If you had to sum up my years on *Full House* in one word, *laughing* would be it. Bob Saget and Dave Coulier were always cracking jokes, many of which were inappropriate for kids, although they were never direct. Our moms were always there, watching from the audience seats even during rehearsals, to make sure nothing crossed the line. I think they thought most of the jokes went over our heads, but I was more mature than my actual age, so I caught on pretty fast. I kept it a secret that I understood most of it, because I didn't want to be excluded from anything.

As you can see, I've had a blast on the set throughout my career, and having a great group of people to work with makes it even better. It was even more enjoyable a few years into the show when my sister Bridgette started working behind the scenes as my stand-in. I think it's telling that my clearest memories from my *Full House* days are of us simply having fun together.

"The Right Stuff"

Though it was fantastic to have adults that made sure I had a great time while working, having fun outside of work as a teen was a must! Because my parents didn't want us kids involved in the Hollywood lifestyle, we didn't go to many industry parties. That didn't really bother me, because I enjoyed spending time with my family and friends at home or doing things other normal teenagers did for entertainment. I wasn't really jealous of the kids who did get to go to the parties because it wasn't something that interested me all that much in the first place. My mom and dad did a good job of talking it down, which just reminds me as a parent that if you say something over and over to your child, it eventually sinks in!

However, my parents did break down and allow us to go to a couple of Hollywood parties when they seemed to really matter to us. The most memorable one for my sisters and me was one that was hosted by *Bop* magazine. The New Kids on the Block were going to be there, and my sisters were dying to meet them. Okay, I'll admit it . . . I was too! Mom and Dad agreed to let us go if Sarah went along with us. Sarah was a college student and was Bridgette and Melissa's homework tutor. She really acted as a mentor to all of us girls. We loved her, she loved us, and our parents obviously trusted her with our lives, because otherwise I don't think they would have agreed to let us go to that party. Bridgette and I were the talk of the set that week, and Andrea Barber (aka Kimmy Gibbler) was totally envious. And that brings me to our current adult obsession with NKOTB. D.J. and Kimmy live on! Andrea and I go to their concert together every time they're in town. And Andrea just ran a 10K with Joey McIntyre as a teammate! Who's jealous now?

So, I didn't go to many parties . . . but what about boys? Aren't boys a big part of a teenage girl's fun? Honestly, I didn't have much time for boys and was very naïve, and I must say that my parents didn't seem too inclined to try to "balance" my life in that area!

My first crush was on Fred Savage (admit it, '80s ladies, he was one of yours too!), but my first non-celebrity crush was a boy from youth group at my church. We would talk on the phone a lot, but it wasn't long before he started making fun of me talking about working. He asked me why I called it "work" or "my job." He said it wasn't really work; it was just fun. I got really defensive about it because while it was fun, it was a lot of work. Most weeks I worked more hours than most adults did. As a result of his attitude, I invited him to come to a taping so he could get a glimpse of what I did every week. In true teenage girl fashion, after I proved my point I no longer had any interest in him.

And because we're still talking boys, I often get asked if I ever had a crush on John Stamos. Truth be told, I didn't, and it's probably because I was so young when the show started. He really was like a cool uncle to me, so thankfully I never had to deal with that weird, awkward phase!

During the final season of *Full House* I met my husband, and then the fun really began . . . but I'll tell you all about that in the next chapter.

Making Room for Fun

So how do I make sure to enjoy life as an adult? Well, a lot of my fun includes Natasha, Lev, and Maks. One of our favorite things to do is having dance parties in the living room. I even bought strobe lights for full effect. You can also often find me singing really loudly and rocking out in the car on our way to school and hockey practice. Trust me, your kids will love this, especially your teenagers! We take videos of just about everything. I love making movies with my kids. Those three write and direct the movies, and after the video has been shot, they're pros at editing the content on our trusty Mac. Our fun also involves a lot of physical activity. We work out together, usually taking twenty-five-minute jogs three times a week before school. That doesn't always seem like a great time to them, but we'll often race to the imaginary finish line, which puts a smile back on their faces! Since we live so close to the ocean, we spend a lot of time at the beach. We ride bikes on the beach path, fly a kite, skim and boogie board, and just dig big holes in the sand and bury each other up to our necks.

Based on my experiences as a child and what I've observed and done as an adult, I believe it's hugely important for adults to do what they can to help balance the lives of the kids for whom they're responsible. Depending on the situation, some kids might need more fun in their lives, while others need less fun and more structure. Each child is different, and each family has its own priorities, so the picture won't always look the same. But all kids need a balance of school, chores, fun, family time, and so on. Too much or too little of one thing can throw everything out of balance and have an adverse effect on the child's development. I'm grateful that I had parents and other adults in my life who were committed to making sure I had balance during my hectic teen years, and I make it a priority now to keep that balance in my own children's lives.

Spending time with my kids makes fun easy for me, but I also enjoy doing things with Val, friends, or even just myself. Fun for me is being able to relax, to which any mom can relate. I enjoy reading a book, watching a movie, having a glass of wine, going for walks, shoe shopping, having lunch dates with Val or a friend, and going dancing. My ultimate fun that isn't so relaxing is racing in 5Ks and 10Ks that involve mud and muscles! Can you say, "cray cray"?

The ways I have fun may not be what would be fun for you, but my point really isn't about *how* to have fun, but rather that as you consider what it looks like to maintain balance in your life, that you should make fun a priority. No, it shouldn't be to the exclusion of other priorities, but that's really the point of balance—all things are in right portion and place. Try to see the humor in everyday situations and you'll be amazed at how easy it is to find everyday tasks fun while still fulfilling all your obligations.

CHAPTER 6

From Russia with Love

Whatever you do, work heartily,
as for the Lord and not for men.
—COLOSSIANS 3:23

• • • • • • • • • • • • • •

Once upon a time there was a little blond-haired Russian boy who started playing hockey when he was three years old. By the time he was five, he and his eight-year-old brother would get on a bus alone at 5:00 a.m. to practice hockey before school every day. Once school was over, they were back on the ice. Hockey, school; school, hockey. That was their life. Those two boys continued to work hard and play hockey until they were NHL stars and Olympic medalists.

On the other side of the world in Los Angeles, a little five-year-old girl, her seven- and ten-year-old sisters, and her eleven-year-old brother would get up and go to school. Many days, after school, the youngest and oldest siblings would go to auditions. Some days they would be on a commercial set all day. Acting, school; school, acting. That was their life. They continued to work hard and went on to act in movies and in two of the most popular TV shows of their time.

Sounds like the beginning of a fairy tale, doesn't it? Well, except in fairy tales it seems as if none of the main characters have a job. These kids were a different story. They knew the value of hard work because they had been doing it for nearly as long as they could remember.

Ecclesiastes 9:10 says, "Whatever your hand finds to do, do it with your might," and that's what Val and I have always done. We work with all our might. We both love to work, and it's actually what helped us really connect when we first met. Some people might say that at points we have each valued work too much, and they might be right. But that doesn't negate the fact that there is much to be said for working hard.

When you think of a creature that works hard, what do you think of? Maybe a seeing-eye dog or a police dog? Perhaps the oxen that helped Pa Ingalls plow the fields? What about bees that make delicious honey? Those are all good examples, but when the Bible talks about working hard, it focuses on ants. Ants? Yes, seriously—ants. "Go to the ant, O sluggard; consider her ways, and be wise. Without having any chief, officer, or ruler, she prepares her bread in summer and gathers her food in harvest" (Prov. 6:6–8). Ants are hard workers. Whatever their task, they do it with all their might, without being forced to do so by someone higher up the chain. The opposite of an ant is a sluggard—a lazy person. The word *sluggard* just sounds bad, doesn't it? I sure don't want to be one, and I never have been, even when I was a teenager.

In the summer of 1994, things were going great for me. *Full House* was as popular as ever, I was finished with high school, and I was looking forward to many more years of hard work in the entertainment industry. Little did I know how everything would change over the next twelve months.

An Adult . . . Finally!

The last year of *Full House* was by far the best year for me, because I was finally an adult! As a kid, you always want to hang out with the older crowd, and I was no exception. Once I turned sixteen and was able to drive myself to the studio, things were really good, but once I finished school it was fantastic. I loved being on the adults' schedule and being a part of their team. It was so great to be able to hang out with Bob, Dave, John, and Lori all day and not have to worry about running back to the school room to finish up homework or study for tests. Although my sister Bridgette was on set with me every day, I was essentially on my own and could make all my own choices.

When I was in school, I would have to learn all of my lines at home, but once I had graduated I could learn my lines during morning rehearsal and blocking time. Plus, not having to study for school made the workweek so much easier. During the weeks when D.J. didn't have a strong presence in the show, I even got a two-hour lunch break. I would head to a restaurant with Bridgette and my other coworkers and take the extra time to browse the Warner Brothers company store or watch the guys from other shows play basketball on the courts behind our stage. "Freedom" is the only word that describes that last season of the show.

If you were a fan of *Full House* back when it was on, you might remember that we didn't know the final season would be our last when we started it. The show was still going strong after seven seasons and we saw no reason to be worried. Nevertheless, one day we were all standing around the set with the executive producers, who explained that the remaining episodes would be our last. Most of us were shocked, to say the least. However, contracts were up after that season, and by that point everyone would have demanded big money. The network could easily bring a new show for much less money and just let *Full House* go out on a high note.

Though I was surprised, I wasn't really upset about the show's cancellation. I was eighteen, I had just entered adulthood, I had moved into my own home, my friends had started college, and I had met a fantastic guy. I felt like the ending of the show was perfect timing for the beginning of a new chapter of my life. So while I was sad that I wouldn't be seeing my second family every day on the set, I was excited to see what life would bring me. I'm an optimistic girl, and I figured I'd quickly move into other jobs. I had always worked hard and I intended to keep doing so; it just wouldn't be with *Full House*. I had total peace and closure about moving on.

Cupid Struck

As I mentioned, I met Val in August of 1994, on the same day I helped Dilini move into college. Dave Coulier had invited the cast to a charity hockey game at the Great Western Forum, where the LA Kings used to play. So that night Bob, John, Lori, Dave, and I headed out for the game. Dave had given me a heads-up that he had met two really great Russian hockey players about my age who would be playing in the game and he wanted to introduce me to them. The older brother, Pavel, was already really famous and the younger brother, Valeri, had just been drafted into the NHL. I don't know why Dave thought about me when he met them the day before, but I suppose God gave him a nudge none of us understood at the time.

I sat with Lori during the game and we both tried to find the Bure brothers on the ice. I saw Pavel go by and tried to get a glimpse of his face through his helmet. Then I saw Val go by and immediately I said to Lori, "I like *that* one!" I loved the way Val's long blond hair blew through the breeze out from under his helmet as he zipped around the ice. I wouldn't say that Val actually had a mullet, since the top of his hair was almost as long as the bottom, but it was definitely a hockey haircut.

After the game, I was introduced to both brothers and Val signed his jersey for me to keep. I was pretty stoked after we left the players' dressing room, and I just kept hoping that I would see him at the after-party so I could talk to him some more.

My friends and I drove over to the Hollywood Park Race Track where the party was in full swing. We rode up the escalator and walked into a sea of people. Most of them were hockey fans, but I was on the lookout for those Russian boys. We walked around, chitchatted, ate some food, and signed autographs, but the Bure brothers were nowhere to be found. I was bummed. After an hour, we decided to leave and I gave up hope of ever seeing Val again. But as we were on our way down the escalator, lo and behold, Val and Pavel were riding up! We all called out to one another, and the two guys rode back down to meet us. Lori was a great wing-woman and encouraged conversation between me and Val—and he asked me for my phone number. I found a pen and paper (which was actually a blank check!) and gave him my digits.

The very next morning the phone rang at 10:00 a.m. My sister answered and yelled, "Candace, there's some guy named Valeri on the phone for you." What? I thought the proper protocol before calling someone was to wait a day or two. I figured this guy must really like me! Val invited me to lunch with him and his brother and we picked a halfway point in Santa Monica on 3rd Street Promenade. After I hung up, I freaked out a little bit. I had never been on a date with a guy I didn't really know and I had no idea what I was supposed to do. I didn't want to go alone because I didn't want to be stuck for conversation in case I clammed up. Neither of my sisters was available to go with me, so I called Lori. I told her the guys invited me to lunch and I really needed her to go along. She agreed to help me out once again.

As we were saying our good-byes after a very nice and casual lunch, Lori asked Val, "So where are you guys staying while you're out here?" He answered, "We've been in Manhattan Beach but we're headed to Northridge today. It's in the Valley." Lori responded, "That's near where Candace lives! Right, Candace? Why don't you guys go for dinner later or meet up since you're so close?" I was utterly embarrassed that she was bold enough to say something so forward, but I was really grateful because I never would have had the courage to do it myself. I guess Lori could read my face well enough to know I was interested in seeing more of Val!

Val and I made plans for him to come to my house at six o'clock that night. Again, since I was super nervous and wanted a plan, I asked my sisters if we could go with them and their boyfriends to have pizza together. Little did I know that Val was planning on picking me up to take me to his family friend's party. But he went along with the pizza plan and didn't say a thing about the missed party until months later. He hadn't wanted to blow our date either.

Val met my parents that night and made a good impression. When he left, my mom said, "My goodness, he's prettier than us girls!" She meant that as a total compliment and we chuckled, but I'll never forget it. When I walked Val to his car and gave him a hug and a wave good-night, I didn't realize that would be the last time I'd see him for months. The NHL was in a lockout that season, but Val was leaving the following morning to head to Fredericton, New Brunswick (on the far eastern side of Canada) to play for the Montreal Canadiens' farm team.

For the next four months, the two of us talked almost every night. In those days before everything was on the Internet, I even forgot what he looked like after awhile because I didn't have a picture of him. Then I finally flew to see him in person right before Christmas. After that, we saw each other more frequently. Since I worked three weeks on, one week off, I started flying out to see him on my weeks off. By June of 1995, we were engaged . . . but that's a story for another chapter.

Bonding over Hard Work

When Val and I first started talking, we would share stories about our childhoods. Our lives were so different. I grew up in Los Angeles. He grew up in the Soviet Union. There was always a meal waiting on the table for me at home. He would often wait in line for eight hours just to get a few rotten tomatoes to share with his mom and brother. My parents had been married for twenty-five years. His parents had divorced when he was young. The differences were endless.

One big thing we had in common was our love of family. Yes, Val's parents were divorced, but his parents were both very involved in raising the two boys. I could tell that Val loved and respected his mother dearly. And his dad, a Russian swimming legend and Olympic medalist, was his hockey training coach. He coached both boys throughout their amateur careers and gave them all the tools they needed to be professional athletes.

Even though we both greatly loved our families, that wasn't our strongest link. We connected instantly when we discovered that we had both been working since the age of five. We were both dedicated to our jobs, and we loved them. We both had a sense of drive, a strong work ethic, direction, and motivation that went beyond that of most people our age. I immediately thought of that youth group boy who thought my job was a joke. This was totally different. Val understood me without me having to explain a thing. It was amazing to have a man my own age in my life that I could bond with over my long work history and my love of hard work.

Working . . . whether You Have a Job or Not

I know that not all of you have jobs, but that doesn't mean you don't—or can't—value hard work. You can work hard at school, sports, serving others, or volunteering in your community or at church. And we all know the extreme effort we have to put in to take care of our family. Colossians 3:23 says, "Whatever you do, work heartily, as for the Lord and not for men." That "whatever you do" doesn't have to mean an actual paid job. If you have one, make it a priority. If you don't, work hard at whatever it is you do. We can learn another important principle from that verse. We are to work hard "for the Lord." Sure, other people will benefit from what we do, and others will see what we do, but ultimately, we are to labor for God. He is the One whose approval we should seek.

When it comes to work, I can't help but think of the woman in Proverbs 31. When I read that chapter in the Bible, it can often make me feel "less than," because what I do is definitely less than what she does. How in the world could any one human do what that woman does? I don't think anyone can do it perfectly, but it's the picture to which we should aspire. There is no doubt the Proverbs 31 woman works hard. Take a look at a few of the things she does: "She rises while it is still night and provides food for her household and portions for her female servants. She evaluates a field and buys it; she plants a vineyard with her earnings. She draws on her strength and reveals that her arms are strong. She sees that her profits are good, and her lamp never goes out at night. . . . She watches over the activities of her household and is never idle" (Prov. 31:15–18, 27 HCSB).

One of the fastest ways to get into trouble is to be idle. Your grandparents may have said to you, "Idle hands are the devil's workshop," and they made a very good—and biblical—point. Second Thessalonians 3:11–12 says, "For we hear that some among you walk in idleness, not busy at work, but busybodies. Now such persons we command and encourage in the Lord Jesus Christ to do their work quietly and to earn their own living." You want to keep your kids out of trouble? Give them something to do. Want to keep yourself from indulging in your "favorite" sin? Get busy doing something worthwhile.

On the typical "God, then family, then work" hierarchy of priorities we have to balance, work seems to get the shaft. But the thing is, working hard is what will help you keep some of your other priorities right. When you put in the necessary time and energy to provide for your family, you are able to do things for and with them that might not be possible without it. And since the Bible has a lot to say about the value of hard work, if you choose to be idle instead, you're not really making God your top priority, because you're not being obedient to Him. See how that works? When we obey God's commands in all parts of our lives, it helps us to keep our priorities in line and keep our lives balanced.

CHAPTER 7

True Companion

*Then the L*ORD *God said, "It is not good for the man to be
alone. I will make a helper as his complement."*
—GENESIS 2:18 (HCSB)

● ● ● ● ● ● ● ● ● ● ● ● ●

D o you believe in Jesus?"
Val and I were riding along in the car one
day after we were engaged, when I started
thinking that we should probably discuss religion. We never
had before, but since we were going to spend the rest of our
lives together and hoped to have children, I knew it had to
be discussed. So, with no warning, I asked him, "Do you
believe in Jesus?"

"Why? Are you not going to marry me if I don't?"

"Just answer me," I said. "Do you believe in Jesus?"

He argued with me a little more about why I wanted to know, but he finally gave in and answered, "Yes, I believe in Jesus."

"Okay," I said. *Phew!* I thought. *We're good then.* And we didn't discuss religion or faith again during our engagement.

There are a ton of issues that couples should discuss before they decide to get married, but I now realize that religion should be very high on that list. Looking back on that little exchange in the car with Val, I laugh at my naïveté about the role of faith in a marriage. I thought that as long as we were both "Christian," we'd be fine.

Even though I wasn't knowingly following the Bible at the time, I can look back and see how God was working through me to prepare our marriage for the day when Val and I would both follow Him with our whole hearts. Some of the things I did are things that most people—no matter their religion—strive to do in their marriage. First and foremost, I knew our relationship had to take priority over that with any other human. And without thinking about it in this way, I realized that not only was my marriage with Val of vital importance, but I had to also create priorities *within* that relationship. There were certain things I needed to do—or not do—in order to show how much I valued Val and our marriage. You'll see what I mean as you read about our engagement and wedding.

A Parisian Proposal

What girl doesn't dream of getting engaged in Paris? Well, I was engaged in the City of Love, and let me tell you that it's not always the romantic situation you imagine in your dreams.

Val and I ended up in Paris by accident. We had meant to go there, but not until later in our European trip. We tried to go to Italy, but Val didn't have the proper visa in his Russian passport, so after a two-day fiasco in an airport "holding room" we ended up in Paris. Needless to say, we were not in a good mood. Both of us were irritated, tired, and cranky, and we got into our first major fight that very evening. I don't even remember what it was about. It wasn't over anything important; we were just two young hotheads that needed to rest.

I was in my own room that night, contemplating whether I should stay or go home, when Val called and asked if we could take a walk and talk things over. As we walked down the Champs-Elysees, we quickly got over our fight. We held hands and laughed as we enjoyed the beauty of our surroundings. All at once Val stopped and pulled out a little box with a ring in it. He told me how much he loved me and wanted to spend the rest of his life with me, and then he asked me to marry him. He put the ring on the ring finger of my right hand, so my first words were, "It's the left one!" followed quickly by, "And yes! Of course I'll marry you!"

Six months earlier, after returning from my first trip to see Val in Canada, a friend had asked me how the trip went and if I liked Val. I told my friend I did like Val, but it wasn't like I was going to marry him. I was only eighteen, after all. Little did I know how our relationship would progress and that two months after I turned the ripe old age of nineteen I wouldn't hesitate to agree to marry the man I "wasn't going to marry." A lot had changed in those six months, not the least of which was the ending of *Full House*. I was ready for a new chapter in my life.

I wasn't, however, ready to tell my parents about the engagement immediately. Dad had only met Val one time— when Val and I had pizza the day after we met. Mom had only seen him one more time when one of my events coincided with one of his hockey games in Washington, D.C. I felt a little guilty that my parents didn't know my fiancé. I didn't want to tell them over the phone, so I decided to wait until we got home just a few days later and tell them over dinner. Thankfully, after the initial shock, they took the news well.

Marrying young didn't make me nervous. My mom was nineteen when she married, my brother was twenty when he got married, and we have a history of long-term marriage in our family. My parents have been married more than forty-four years, my dad's parents were married more than sixty-five years, and my mom's parents have been married more than sixty-seven years!

So age wasn't a factor when Val and I decided to get married. I felt like I had lived a whole lot of life in my mere nineteen years, and Val, too, was mature for his age of twenty-one. He wasn't into the typical twenties party scene; he was ready to start a family and have a wife and kids to come home to after he was on the road playing hockey. Some people assume that I got married young because of my Christian faith and was "waiting" to have sex until I was married, since years earlier I had professed I would do so. But the truth was, my relationship with God was the last thing on my mind and I had no problem living with Val—despite my parents' disappointment—for a year before we got married.

I had no idea that Val was going to propose that day or even while we were on that trip. After a few months of dating he had told me he really loved me and was going to get a ring, but I thought he was joking. It turns out that he really did buy the ring after just a few months and was waiting for that trip to pop the question. We had never really talked about marriage until he asked me to marry him on that starry Parisian night.

I, Candace, Take You, Val

On the morning of June 22, 1996, my mom, attendants, and I headed to my hairdresser's salon to get ready for my big day. Dilini, of course, was my maid of honor. My sisters and friend Shelene served as bridesmaids. We spent all day primping at the Jim Wayne Salon and then hopped into a limo to head to the church to get dressed. Meanwhile, Val and his best man, brother Pavel, were off playing tennis, arriving at the church just minutes before the ceremony started. They didn't have time to take proper photos together, so the only photo we have of them together was of them drinking smoothies in the alley behind the church. Way to go, guys!

The wedding was held at the church in Van Nuys, California, where I had attended in my later teen years. Val liked the stained glass windows because they reminded him of the more traditional churches that he was used to in Russia. He actually didn't care if we were married in a church or not, but it was super important to me, even though my faith wasn't a top priority at the time.

When my dad walked me down the aisle, we couldn't look at each other because he was already crying before it even started and I didn't want to be a mess before I got to the altar. Val and I said our vows in front of 120 family members and friends (including most of my *Full House* family). Val's immediate family was there, but some Russian guests were unsuccessful with getting visas to attend, which was a disappointment. As a result, most of the guests were my own friends and family, most of whom had never even met Val. We exchanged rings, listened to Mark Cohn's "True Companion," and I jumped up and down and squealed in excitement when the pastor pronounced us husband and wife. Then we headed off to our reception at the Sherwood Country Club in Westlake, where we ate, danced, and enjoyed spending time with our guests.

Our wedding was simple by today's standards, but it was perfect. Even though we were both financially secure and held some celeb status, we had no desire to be extravagant. Val didn't care much about the actual wedding day festivities because they weren't celebrated the same way in Russia, so we decided to set a reasonable budget for our special day.

Val did, however, want to be involved in the planning and help make each decision. We had hired a wedding coordinator, but she was mostly just there for the day of the event, not to help me plan it. I did it all myself, not because I'm a control freak, but because my dad had always taught me to do things for myself, and my wedding was no exception. I did forget to do one thing that I wish I had done—providing a small gift for each guest at the reception tables.

But other than that, I think I did a pretty good job! So I did the planning, and Val definitely had an opinion about everything. Thankfully he was fine with me just narrowing everything down to a couple of choices, and then we would make the final decision together.

A Respectful Balance

Making wedding decisions with Val was my first glimpse into how our relationship would work in terms of life together as husband and wife. For the first time I saw my future husband's leadership role in our family. It always made me chuckle that he wanted to be part of every decision for a ceremony he really didn't care much about.

Val even had an opinion about our personalized thank-you cards. He didn't think it was right for my name to be first on the cards. He fought for his name first, thinking that since he was the man of the house, it should read: Valeri and Candace Bure. So we got into an etiquette discussion with our wedding coordinator, and she guided us to eventually come to a compromise of ordering half of the cards with his name first and the other half with my name first, regardless of which way was right. The funny part of it was that he didn't intend on writing any of the cards himself; that was my job. I sent all of his family and friends' thank-you notes on the cards with his name first.

I really appreciated the coordinator's advice to meet in the middle, and there have been a string of those decisions in our lives together. Some would call it an ego issue, but I saw it as my initial lesson in making my husband feel respected, even with something as "small" as a thank-you card. It was one of the first examples of how I showed the world that my husband is my priority in our relationship. People talk about marriage being a 50-50 give-and-take situation, but it's more than that. It's more than compromise. It's about giving 100 percent, finding your role in that relationship and honoring all aspects of it.

My husband is a natural-born leader. I quickly learned that I had to find a way of honoring his take-charge personality and not get frustrated about his desire to have the final decision on just about everything. I am not a passive person, but I chose to fall into a more submissive role in our relationship because I wanted to do everything in my power to make my marriage and family work. I had watched my parents' relationship over the years and had seen their example of doing what needed to be done to make the marriage work. I knew I needed to do whatever it took to stay in sync with Val and not build any bitterness because of our equally strong personalities.

Before the hair on your neck stands up straight, don't think for a second that I get walked all over. I don't. I have always firmly voiced my opinion, but when it comes down to us ultimately not agreeing on something, I submit to his leadership. That decision to submit originally had nothing to do with my Christian faith, because it wasn't strong at the time. But once I started understanding marriage from a biblical perspective it all made sense. I now recognize that I do all things in my marriage for the Lord. He is my ultimate priority, and I honor God when I honor my husband, whether or not Val deserves my honor or respect at the time.

The Bible is very clear about what husbands and wives should strive toward in their relationship. Ephesians 5:33 says, "Let each [husband] love his wife as himself, and let the wife see that she respects her husband." Is that always an easy thing to do? No, it's not easy from either person's perspective. But it is vastly important. When a man feels like his wife doesn't respect him, it basically makes him feel like he's a failure or less of a man. A man desires his wife's respect just as much as a woman desires her husband's love. The way I think about it is this: When I don't show respect to my husband, he feels the same way I do when he doesn't show love to me. On the other hand, when I *do* show him respect, his emotional reaction is the same as mine is when he shows me I'm the love of his life. That is great motivation for me to respect my husband.

As husband and wife, Val and I are "one flesh" (Gen. 2:24). We are no longer two people, but one. With this in mind, it only stands to reason that our relationship should be the most important relationship we have with anyone other than God. Keeping that relationship strong and healthy is of vast importance, and I know that respecting Val is the best way I can make sure that happens. And, in turn, he realizes that he needs to love me unconditionally.

I know that if my husband ends his day feeling disrespected because of something I did or didn't do, then my priorities in marriage are out of line and things are seriously out of balance. That means I need to take a step back and reevaluate what is most important to me. Is it more important for me to be "right" or "get the last word" or simply do what I want to do regardless of his feelings or input, or is it more important for my husband to feel cherished and respected? There are definitely times when I choose my own needs above Val's, but in the end, I know that I must put him first.

Showing respect to Val has to be my top priority in my marriage. I am glad I learned this principle early, because I know it has saved us a lot of heartache over the years. I do still fail at times, and when I do, Val forgives me and so does

God. I'm so grateful that both my husband and my heavenly Father give me second (and third . . . and hundredth) chances.

This issue of respect in marriage might be a new concept for some of you. If it is, I want to challenge you to try it. I can't promise that it will solve all of your problems, but I can tell you that it can go a long way toward strengthening your relationship. In fact, it may just be the best thing that ever happened to your marriage.

CHAPTER 8

Oh, Canada

*"Rebekah is here in front of you. Take her and go, and let
her be a wife for your master's son, just as the Lord has
spoken." . . . Then Rebekah and her female servants got up,
mounted the camels, and followed the man.*

—Genesis 24:51, 61 (HCSB)

• • • • • • • • • • • • • •

I magine being in love and marrying your dream man
in front of friends and family and being so excited
about what the future will bring. Do you see it?
Maybe you've already been there or are still looking forward
to that day. Now imagine life a few months later. You're still
married to your dream man, but things aren't quite as exciting. After living in the same place your entire life, you now
live in a different country. Your friends and family members

and the only life you've ever known are all thousands of miles away. That dream husband is still dreamy, but his job takes him away from home several nights a week for much of the year. You've worked for fifteen years, and all of a sudden you don't have a job. You don't feel like you fit in with your husband's coworkers' wives. You're lonely and a bit depressed, and so what do you do? Well, if you're me, you sit on the couch, watch soap operas, and eat until you make yourself sick.

Whether you're married or not, you recognize that marriage brings a huge amount of change into people's lives. For many, some core parts of their lives will stay the same. They stay in the same city, in the same job, with the same friends and family nearby, and so on. Of course, the marriage itself will bring many changes, but a good part of the person's life structure stays the same. For others, though, marriage changes much, much more.

Rebekah was one such woman. We read in Genesis 24 that one day she was innocently filling a water jar at a well, and the next day she was whisked off to marry an unknown man in a faraway land. Of course, it doesn't seem Rebekah had any choice in the matter, but what's to say she wouldn't have done it anyway? Regardless, everything changed for Rebekah in a heartbeat. She left behind everything she knew in order to get married.

I know many of you can relate to Rebekah. Maybe you, too, left behind everything you knew to marry the man you love. You might have deployed on an overseas military assignment. Perhaps you ventured into the great unknown to serve God as a missionary on the other side of the world. Some of you have had your entire lives uprooted due to a job transfer, an ailing parent, or simply the call of God to go somewhere new. Even if you haven't had to move to a new place, you've likely experienced another huge life change. You know what it's like to feel as if nothing in life is familiar.

Do you know what can easily happen when you find yourself in a completely new situation? Your priorities can get out of whack. You don't know what you're doing or what you should be doing. You're surrounded by new people and new opportunities. And your life becomes unbalanced because you're overwhelmed, because there *aren't* many things to balance anymore, or because they're so new you don't even know where or how to begin.

You've been there, and I've been there. There have been seasons in my life when I wasn't able to keep my life balanced, and my first few years of marriage are a good example of that inability.

From Actress to Hockey Wife

When Val and I got engaged I was excited about starting a new chapter in my life. *Full House* had just ended, I had grown up right along with my alter ego D.J., and I was ready to move on to a grand new adventure. However, my adventure led me thousands of miles from home to Montreal, Canada.

I can definitely relate to the biblical Rebekah. Though it was by my own choice, I suddenly found myself in a new country with no friends, no family nearby, and essentially no job. My husband had an exciting career, but during the hockey season he was gone half of the time. I knew nothing about this new life as a housewife, and I had no sense of balance because I had left behind everything that was familiar to me.

I didn't consider asking Val to move to L.A. It wasn't an option for him if he wanted to continue to play in the NHL. He couldn't very well demand a trade to the Los Angeles Kings. He played for the Montreal Canadiens, so we needed to live in Montreal. It also didn't occur to me to ask him, "Would you consider not working? Would you give up playing hockey so I can stay in L.A. and work?" I was marrying a professional athlete, for goodness sake. What twenty-year-old woman wouldn't love that? I certainly did, and it was definitely part of the attraction.

It's not that I didn't want to work, because I did. I had been working my whole life, and I couldn't imagine not doing so in the future. I figured the opportunities would be there and I would fly to L.A. whenever I got auditions and it would all work out. However, things were a little tougher than I had thought they would be. I did work on a couple of TV movies before I got pregnant with Natasha, but life as a hockey wife wasn't really what I had imagined it would be and was nothing like what I was used to.

Have you ever trained or worked toward something your whole life, only to eventually be kept from doing it? As much as I was looking forward to my new role as wife, cheerleader, and homemaker, I felt like the wind had been knocked out from me when I couldn't work anymore. It's not that I found my value or worth from my work, but it was a creative outlet, a part of me that God specifically designed that was suddenly gone. It felt like I lost a piece of me.

At the time, Montreal was a hot spot for making movies, but I couldn't just simply audition and get offered a job there. Because of my American citizenship, I couldn't work without a visa, and with taxes and residency issues it all became very complicated. I thought about volunteering at a hospital or nonprofit organization, but I was easily recognizable and any help I could have given would have been more trouble for them than it was worth.

So things weren't working out the way I wanted them to on the job front, and friendships were a little difficult to establish too. I wasn't sure what the other hockey wives thought about me. Walking into the wives' room after my first games was almost frightening. I don't think I had seen so much Chanel, Versace, and Louis Vuitton in Hollywood. The women were nice, but I felt like a teenager playing grown up, and even though I'd traveled the world and was mature, it didn't make me feel any more confident when I was there. Being a celebrity made it even more uncomfortable and it was hard to find my place. Some of the ladies were veterans, having husbands who'd been in the league for years. Others were players' girlfriends, and it was easy to see the difference between a high school sweetheart and a short-term girlfriend. I didn't quite fit in with any of them. My insecurities and shyness were sometimes interpreted as arrogant, but I managed to make a few new buddies quickly by asking simple questions about where the cool places were to eat or shop. Eventually those questions turned into asking where to find a good dry cleaner, grocery store, or gym. Though I knew it would take some time, I kept plugging away at trying to establish friendships.

I think one of the hardest things about moving is the relationship aspect. You leave friends behind and you have to make new ones in your new city. Some of the old pals will prove to be lifelong friends, as will some of the new ones. But I've discovered that much of the emotional turmoil connected with moving is the loss or changing of relationships. When I moved to Canada, I still had my family and friends in California that I could talk to on the phone and visit on occasion, but I really missed being around people who really knew me. There's something about being in the physical presence of those who know you well that lifts you up more than just talking on the phone can often do. We all need friends who can be there for us in person, to see how we're doing, to do things for and with us, and to hold us accountable when we start to stray off the right path. It can be scary to put ourselves out there, but if we don't, we won't know what we're losing out on.

Food Is Not the Answer

As a result of my insecurities about work, a lack of good friends nearby, and the huge life changes I had recently experienced, I became lonely and depressed. On a typical day I would get up, sit around the house for awhile, work out, eat lunch with Val if he wasn't on the road, watch soap operas in the afternoons, sit around some more, and eat.

If you've read my first book, *Reshaping It All*, you know my battle with bulimia began during those early days in Montreal. My eating disorder was not based on body image issues or a desire to lose weight. You would assume that I had been pressured about my weight during *Full House*, but I wasn't. Perhaps my mom shielded me from any potential dangers, or maybe everyone was just fine with me being cute little chubby-cheeked D.J. Tanner. Whatever the case, bulimia wasn't a Hollywood issue for me. It was simply my way of coping with adjustment and fear *after* I left Hollywood and wasn't sure who I was anymore. My life was unrecognizable, so I tried to find emotional comfort in food.

To some extent, we all have an emotional relationship with food. Many people are able to keep that relationship a healthy one; I was not one of those fortunate souls. At first I only did it when Val was on the road, like it was an illicit affair. I would sit alone in front of the TV in our apartment and simply eat. I would eat and eat and eat until I was disgusted with myself. In order to alleviate the guilt and disgust I felt at my binging, I would purge. I let my emotions dictate what I ate. Can you relate? Do you eat cake when you're happy? Maybe you scarf down a carton of ice cream when you're lonely, or you gorge yourself on candy when you're bored.

With most things we do in secret, we get bolder and more wrapped up in what we're doing, and we eventually get caught. My dad was the one who discovered my secret shame, and I was distraught by how much it hurt him to see me in such pain and confusion. I had never intended for my actions to hurt my loved ones, but they had. The discovery—and the embarrassment and shame that went along with it—was one of the turning points in my battle with bulimia, but my emotional struggles with food still cropped up.

Strong emotions can lead us to do things we wouldn't normally do. In my loneliness, I recognized that I had a void in my life, I tried to fill it with food, and I became a slave to that food. What I didn't realize then was that the only thing that could truly satisfy me and break the bonds of my unhealthy habit was a relationship with Jesus Christ. Instead of turning to food for comfort, I should have been turning to God. He is our ultimate source of joy, freedom, strength, calm, healing, and comfort. He will deliver us from the things that hold us captive, as we read in Psalm 18:2: "The Lord is my rock and my fortress and my deliverer, my God, my rock, in whom I take refuge, my shield, and the horn of my salvation, my stronghold."

I've also learned that God has an interest in what or how we eat. We rarely think about this, because everyone has to eat. It's a necessary part of life that we just take for granted. But God does care about what we eat and He desires to be present in that aspect of our lives. He wants us to be healthy, and He wants us to be self-disciplined not just in our eating habits but in all that we do. I was not disciplined in eating; in fact, I was committing the sin of gluttony. I needed to make better choices in order to be obedient to God and to live a healthier life.

If you or someone you know is struggling with an eating disorder, please tell a friend and seek help. It is not healthy physically, mentally, emotionally, or spiritually. Eating disorders and the abuse of food will slowly destroy you, and if it goes on too long it can prove fatal. I do not wish that for anyone. There is help, and there is freedom from this food slavery. Do whatever you need to do to move toward a healthier lifestyle.

The Foundation of Balance

During those early years of marriage, I had no foundation and no sense of direction or purpose, which is what made identifying what I should be balancing so difficult—and you really need to know what your priorities should be in order to balance them. Though I did seem to have more direction in my life once I had my kids, I didn't really feel like I had a firm foundation to stand on until I truly began to follow Jesus Christ, the true foundation. First Corinthians 3:11 says, "For no one can lay a foundation other than that which is laid, which is Jesus Christ." Anything we try to use as a foundation—whether it's work, food, another person, or anything else—will ultimately fail. It might seem to work for a time, but it won't last. Only Jesus will last, and He will be there not just for this lifetime, but also for eternity.

If you find yourself in a similar state of an unbalanced life, I encourage you to go to Jesus to find a sense of stability, direction, purpose, and balance. He will guide you where you need to be. He will help you reorder your priorities, evaluate your life, and create a sense of balance for you and those who depend on you.

The fact that I am writing a book about balance does not mean that I always have it all together. I don't. Sometimes I get too caught up in one aspect of my life and the neglect of others. It's not uncommon for me to find myself putting work at a higher priority than it should be. Other times I get so busy that friendships take a back seat. But it usually doesn't take long before I realize it or one of my friends or family members points it out to me. (You have to love accountability!) And if it takes me too long, something will happen that I just know is God telling me to stop and take stock of what I'm doing.

When I recognize that things are spinning out of control and nothing is in balance, the first thing I do is pray and read God's Word. Philippians 4:6–7 says, "Do not be anxious about anything, but in everything by prayer and supplication with thanksgiving let your requests be made known to God. And the peace of God, which surpasses all understanding, will guard your hearts and your minds in Christ Jesus." I often feel like a failure when I realize that I'm not living the way God wants me to, but God always brings me peace, gives me the reassurance that He loves me, and helps me to think clearly so that I can begin to get things back on track. God doesn't "magically" just make things okay, though. I have to work at it, but if I ask Him, He will give me the strength and ability to make wise decisions about where my priorities should be and how I need to keep things balanced for myself and for my family.

CHAPTER 9

Home Is Where
the Heart Is

*Trust in the L*ORD *with all your heart, and do not rely on*
your own understanding; think about Him in all your ways,
and He will guide you on the right paths.
—P<small>ROVERBS</small> 3:5–6 (<small>HCSB</small>)

• • • • • • • • • • • • • •

I
f you want to start a fight and end friendships, initi-
ate a debate about working moms versus stay-at-home
moms in a room with a mixed crowd. There's not
much that can get a mom more fired up than to have someone tell her that her decision to work or to stay home with
the kids is the wrong choice.

I'm not here to try to win you over to one side or the
other. I've lived on both sides, and I've loved and disliked

aspects of both. When it came down to it, each decision was about evaluating our situation in that specific time and season of my life and figuring out what I needed to do in order to create the best sense of balance I could within my family. I've learned that with God's help, I can always discover the best path to take. He will open and close the right doors if I trust Him and seek His wisdom and guidance.

Some of you have already had to make that decision; others will have to make it soon, and still others may never have to make it. Whichever situation you're in, I believe this chapter has something for you. Hopefully it will give you a better understanding of how the uniqueness of each individual and family is what drives their decisions in all aspects of life. We are all different, and we should make the wisest decisions possible and do the best we can with what God has given us.

And Baby Makes Three . . . and Four . . . and Five

Val and I made the decision to have kids while we were young, so in 1998, two years after we were married, Natasha was born. Just as she was in my womb, Natasha came out fighting after twenty-two hours of labor. But, my goodness, was she ever beautiful! She looked like a little porcelain doll with her eyes wide open. And still at fifteen years old, she can be as sweet and precious as ever, but she will fight to the death over whatever she's after.

Lev came along in 2000, cool as a cucumber with a scrunchy, pudgy face. He was a shocking difference compared to Natasha and I don't know that he opened his eyes for a few days. It looked like he ate a sour lemon and couldn't get rid of the aftertaste! However, it didn't take long for him to grow into his good looks with those striking blue eyes, blonde hair, and muscular lean build. He definitely takes after his dad! If Val thinks he's going to have it tough with Natasha's boyfriends, I'll be equally as passionate warding off the girls after Lev's heart.

Two years later Maks rounded out our family of five. My "baby" came into the world as the smallest of the three, but he is now not only physically the biggest but he also has the biggest and liveliest personality. Maks was the baby you just wanted to squeeze all day long. He was always happy and super chill, and with his enormous head, huge blue eyes, and chubby arm and leg rolls, you couldn't help but want to eat him up. I've been told several times that Maks would make the perfect politician because he could talk you into anything with his engaging storytelling, charm, and wit. I'm definitely praying over that one!

Weighing the Options

The year Natasha was born Val was traded to the Calgary Flames, so I found myself uprooted once more. Not long after Natasha's birth I started meeting with agents in L.A. to try and restart my career after my pregnancy. I was ready to feel like myself again and throw my energy into the thing that had defined me for most of my life—my work.

Even though I wanted to be there for my kids like my mom had, the thought of not acting anymore wasn't something I wanted to consider. It was all I knew, I was good at it, and I really enjoyed it. I didn't want to give it up, and at first I really didn't think I would have to. I had read the stories in magazines about women who were doing it all and seemingly with a perfect balance. Women were supposed to be empowered and have it all, so that's what I decided I was going to do. I would be superwoman.

I took Natasha with me on my trips to L.A., where we would stay at my parents' house so they could help out and look after her. On one particular ten-day trip when I had meetings and auditions all day long, I'd come home each night after Natasha was already in bed. I realized by day five that something had to change. I was far away from my husband and I wasn't able to spend time with my baby girl. It just wasn't going to be possible for Val to work in one city, me to work in another city in another *country*, and at the same time take care of Natasha and give her any sense of stability. I wanted to work, but more than that, I wanted to be there for my kids and my husband. It's what my mom had done, so it was a natural conclusion for me, even if it meant I had to give up my dream of being superwoman.

When I approached Val about this, I found out he was on the same page as I was and had been hoping that I'd come to the same conclusion. He supported my dreams, but he also wanted our family to be the top priority. Since we both had unique careers that were based in different cities, we couldn't both do our jobs and have the kind of family life that we wanted.

Basically, Val and I made the decision that I would stay home out of a sense of conviction that it was really the only viable option for us. In order for our little family to continue to function we had no choice but for one of us to stay home with our children. If we didn't make that decision, our priorities would have to shift in ways we didn't want them to and it would basically throw our lives into chaos. One of us needed to put our career on hold, and that wasn't an option for Val. Professional hockey careers are short enough as it is. I wouldn't have dreamed of asking him to sacrifice his brief career in order to pursue my own. Besides, I'm a woman, and it's in my God-given nature to be the nurturer and caretaker at home. At the time, though, I wasn't really following God or seeking His will in my life. Consulting Him wasn't really part of my decision-making strategy. With that in mind, I still believe He guided Val and me in our decision, even if we didn't know it at the time.

A Difficult Transition

While the decision to stay home with my kids was a logical one and was the right choice for our family at the time, it wasn't an easy decision or transition for me. So much of who I saw myself to be (and who the world saw me to be) was wrapped up in my work. It felt like the wind was knocked out of me when fans would come up asking me what my next project was, only to look at me sadly when I told them I was now a stay-at-home mom. Being an actress was all I had ever known; it was work and career that drew Val and me together and was definitely a priority for both of us.

When I made that decision to stay home with my kids, it was a decision I knew I was going to have to live with every day for a long time. Unless Val's career ended suddenly, I had to come to terms with the fact that I wasn't going to work again for many years. It was a major disappointment for me, and I felt guilty about that. I know some of you can relate to those feelings. Like me, you're more driven toward work than home. But I have finally come to realize that I don't need to feel guilty about the way God made me. The Bible says I am "fearfully and wonderfully made" (Ps. 139:14). God gave me the drive to work. Of course, not everything we are inclined to do is a good thing. We all have sinful desires, but the desire to work isn't one of them. The Bible has many positive things to say about hard work. And, as is true with everything—it's about how we balance all that God has created and called us to be and do.

The fact that I was disappointed that I wouldn't have a job for potentially many years doesn't mean I didn't love my children. Of course I love my children and want to take care of them. That simply has nothing to do with also loving to work. I had to surrender to the fact that that part of me wouldn't be fulfilled for a season of my life. Sometimes making the right choice means not loving everything that results from that decision. Giving up work was a sacrifice I had to make in order to make the best decision for my family at that time.

It took me two years to really surrender to motherhood and lay down my career dreams. Once I let that go and embraced my new path, I started to enjoy being a stay-at-home mom. I only wish I had enjoyed it more from the very beginning.

Even though it started out a bit rough, I'm so grateful that I made the choice and had the opportunity to be a full-time mom for a season. During those ten years I grew a lot in my faith and my relationship with the Lord, and I believe that's due to the fact that I wasn't trying to juggle too many things. The fewer balls we have up in the air, the easier it is to keep them all moving simultaneously in the air. Because of the choice to stay home with the kids instead of trying to work in a different city than my husband, I was better able to keep balance in my life and in my husband's and kids' lives.

Embracing Uniqueness

God gives us all different desires and goals for our lives. Some of us dream of staying home with our families and others fantasize about an amazing, fulfilling career. Neither of those desires is wrong. What we each need to determine, though, is how God wants us to balance those aspects of our lives. Any mother will have to do both (even if she's not paid to work), and it's important to discern God's will in these areas.

When we look again to the Proverbs 31 woman, she is both working and taking care of her family. There are many verses throughout that section about the virtuous wife that show her working. "She seeks wool and flax, and works with willing hands. She is like the ships of the merchant; she brings her food from afar" (vv. 13–14). "She perceives that her merchandise is profitable. Her lamp does not go out at night" (v. 18). "She makes bed coverings for herself; her clothing is fine linen and purple" (v. 22). "She makes linen garments and sells them; she delivers sashes to the merchant" (v. 24).

And just when you're thinking this is about the virtuous *wife*, not the virtuous *mother*, I urge you to keep reading! "She looks well to the ways of her household and does not eat the bread of idleness. Her children rise up and call her blessed; her husband also, and he praises her" (vv. 27–28). This woman is a wife, a mother, a worker, a nurturer, a businesswoman, an organizer . . . the list could go on and on. The point is that she balances all of those things. Does she do it perfectly? Well, if she's human, then the answer is no. None of us can balance and prioritize our lives perfectly all the time. But this woman knows the value of all of those different aspects of herself and her life and she embraces them even as she likely struggles to keep all of the plates spinning.

God gives us each various talents, strengths, and weaknesses, and He has put each of us in a unique situation. There is no cookie-cutter answer to whether a mother should work outside the home, and my prayer is that women would stop calling each other out and support each other instead. At the same time, I hope we can all remember that we are accountable to God and to our families, not to other women. In Proverbs God gives us an example of a woman who is doing it all *and* is being called blessed by the people she serves. If God wasn't pleased with her choices, I don't think we would be reading such great things about her!

I have a dear friend in Florida who has five elementary- and middle-school-aged children, is a high-profile attorney who had a TV call-in show for fifteen years, has been a nationally syndicated radio talk show host, and also holds a pilot's license and a psychology degree. Does she have help? Yes! But she prioritizes the daily chores and life's events that are most necessary and meaningful when it comes to pouring into, teaching, and training her children each day.

Being supermom doesn't mean you have to be everything to your child. For example, you don't have to be your child's homework helper if it's a source of stress and you're able to supplement it with a tutor or an older child who can explain it better! Household chores are a must, and something our children need to be taught to do, but if you're able to afford help in this area, why wouldn't you if it allows you to use the time for something else that's important to you? You don't have to feel guilty about it when it helps relieve a burden so that you are free to invest in those things God has created and enabled you to uniquely do. I would love a full-time housekeeper, which I don't have, but I do have a cleaning woman who comes twice a week for four hours. Val and I feel our money is well spent in this area and are willing to sacrifice other "wants"—not needs—in order to have her help.

And while we're at it, let's talk nannies. I'll be the first to admit it's been a word I've rolled my eyes at when ladies talked about theirs, much to my shame. I totally confess any arrogance I've had toward someone who's had a nanny when I've proudly said I didn't. Why did I ever think women who have a nanny seemed snotty or spoiled to have one? Over time and maturity, I have seen the truth about the value of nannies for some families. Although I've never had a nanny, I've used babysitters throughout my children's lives. Just because they're not here every day doesn't mean they're not working for my family. And what about Grandma and Grandpa? If they watch your baby two or three days each week in the mornings, isn't that having help with childcare? Some of us don't have the good fortune of having family close by, so nannies become a valid resource. I've seen nannies who've been with families for years and they become like an aunt or a grandma to the children they watch. As a mom who has a lot on her plate, I understand how the help of a consistent person in kids' lives is valuable.

On the other end of the spectrum from my friend in Florida, my sister Melissa is a full-time stay-at-home mom who homeschools her four children, and my sister-in-law Chelsea does the same with her six kids. And neither of them could imagine doing it any other way. I give major props to those women whose hearts' desire is to dedicate their whole lives to their families without the distraction of a formal job. Being a mom *is* a full-time job and you don't have to get paid to prove it. I probably have more homeschooling/ stay-at-home mom friends than working ones, and while I would love to have a heart that is inclined to do that, I simply don't. And I've learned that it's okay.

We need to recognize that other women are just as capable of deciding what is best for their families as we are for ours. What is right for one family might not be right for another, but that doesn't mean it's wrong for that first family. Doing it uniquely and differently is okay when your ultimate goal is to do it all unto the Lord. This is where having a perspective bent toward seeking balance is helpful. It keeps us from creating hard "musts" where the Bible really hasn't given us such cookie-cutter models. A focus on balancing all the priorities given to us from God is what we see in the life of the woman in Proverbs 31.

The writer of Proverbs ends the final chapter better than I could ever end my own on this topic: "Charm is deceitful, and beauty is vain, but a woman who fears the LORD is to be praised. Give her of the fruit of her hands, and let her works praise her in the gates" (Prov. 31:30–31). Like the Proverbs 31 woman, let your works bring praise at the city gate.

CHAPTER 10

On the Road Again

"I have told you these things so that in Me you may have
peace. You will have suffering in this world.
Be courageous! I have conquered the world."

—John 16:33 (HCSB)

• • • • • • • • • • • • •

As I write this chapter, a tragedy has recently occurred that shocked the nation. A gunman entered an elementary school in Newtown, Connecticut, and murdered twenty-six innocent children and adults. It is something that has horrified us all, but it is also something that has helped us to reevaluate our priorities in life. I know tragedies happen worldwide every day, and they happen on a smaller scale in the U.S. every day, but we don't often hear about them. On the one hand

I don't want a daily reminder of the horrors that humans are capable of committing and the suffering that inevitably follows. But on the other hand, they do help us to remember what is most important in life—namely our faith and our families.

When events such as the Newtown shootings take place, we all take stock of our relationships with our family members and with God. We want to make sure our family relationships are strong and healthy. We tend to find it easier to forgive past wrongs and make commitments to be kinder, gentler, more compassionate, and simply better spouses, children, parents, and siblings. Tragedies also typically draw us closer to God. While we may ask why He allows terrible things to happen, we also somehow realize that He is the only One who can really help us through it and give us the peace we need. Only He can make things new and whole again.

One thing we realize when disaster strikes is that life must go on. I don't want to make light of tragedies and suffering, but whether they happen to us or we just hear about them, we still must make the daily decisions that make up our lives. Even through the pain, numbness, or incredulity, we must complete the mundane tasks of living as well as carry on with huge life changes.

September 11, 2001, was a day that reminded me that life must go on even in the midst of disaster. Like I'm sure it did for all of you, it made me draw closer to my family. It made me want to shield the ones I love from pain and heartbreak. It made me thankful that I have a God who loves me, and it made me want to follow Him more closely. But the events of 9/11 also happened in the midst of a huge life change for my family.

Moving in the Midst of Tragedy

On September 13, 2001, my family was supposed to move from Calgary, Alberta, to South Florida, a distance of about 3,000 miles. Our belongings and cars had already been packed up and shipped, but my husband, two toddlers, and I needed to get our dogs, our personal items, and ourselves to Florida so Val could start training camp with his new team, the Florida Panthers. My mom and sister had also come to help pack up and take care of the kids during the move, since I was nearly seven months pregnant with Maks. We were all supposed to just hop on a plane and get there within the course of a day. But, as you remember, all flights were stopped after 9/11, and we had no idea when they would start back up. Not getting to Florida on time for training camp wasn't an option, so the grueling process of figuring out plan B went into full effect.

It was hard to be frustrated by the situation, because we fully understood the reason why, and we were still in a sense of shock over what had happened. However, we also knew that we still had obligations and responsibilities to fulfill. Val had to get to his new job, and we weren't sure how we were going to be able to get there. Even if we could have gotten Val to Florida and come later ourselves, we didn't want to take that option. After the events of the past few days, we wanted our family to be together. Who knew what else might happen? We needed a solution, and we needed one fast.

As has happened many times in my life, one of my managers came up with a solution that would help us all stay together and get to Val's new job on time. He found us a tour bus. Yes, that's right—a tour bus, just like rock stars use. We had two drivers, so they could take turns driving and sleeping and we could pretty much go nonstop.

So we loaded up the kids and dogs and set out for Florida in our tour bus. It took us about forty-eight hours to get there, which included stops every four to five hours so the kids and dogs could run around for awhile. Somewhere along the way, one of our drivers discovered that I had never had a Krispy Kreme donut, so we pulled the bus over to allow me to indulge in that little piece of heaven. I also had my first meal at Cracker Barrel as we drove through the South.

I can only imagine what the neighbors thought when we pulled into our gated community in the tour bus and parked in our cul-de-sac. They quickly discovered that we weren't rock stars, but I was a little curious about how they would respond to having a grown-up D.J. Tanner and a professional hockey player living down the street. As God would have it, He put us next door to a hockey-loving family who are now lifelong friends, and the rest of the street was filled with the best neighbors one could ever have.

New Neighbors, New Friends

When we found out Val had been traded to the Florida Panthers, we were ecstatic. Val's brother Pavel played for the Panthers, so we would be living near family for the first time in our married lives. And I was excited because it was warm and sunshiny in Florida. I didn't care that I didn't know anyone there; I just wanted to be warm. Don't get me wrong, I enjoyed the cities where we lived in Canada and got to know so many great people there. But I'm a California girl and I like my warm weather, so after nearly seven years of cold Canadian winters, I was ready for Florida.

After we got the call about the trade during the summer of 2001, Val and I went to Florida to find a house. We had spent four days looking and couldn't find one. There was one area I really wanted to look at, but our realtor kept telling us it wasn't a great location for us and she didn't know why I kept wanting to go there. I had heard really good things about it and kept pressing her, but she kept showing us houses in other areas. Finally, our time was up and we hadn't found a house. Val and I said we would extend our trip by one more day if she would show us properties in the area I wanted. She finally agreed, and the first home we walked into on that final day was the one we bought.

There was a clubhouse in our new neighborhood, and soon after we moved in we started playing tennis and working out at the gym and meeting people. Everyone was so nice and helpful. I was so grateful that our new neighbors welcomed us with open arms . . . and open doors. I had never lived somewhere that people would just "pop by" unexpectedly like they did in our Florida neighborhood. In fact, I had never lived anywhere that I even knew my neighbors. It was a little unsettling at first, but I quickly grew to really enjoy our close-knit community.

My first experience with this new, extremely friendly and neighborly culture was with my neighbor Debbie, who lived several blocks over. She came over within a week or two of our arrival and brought homemade cookies to welcome us to the neighborhood. My garage door had been open, so she came to that door instead of my front door, which was unusual to me. She also mentioned that if I needed anything during my pregnancy, like someone to pick up groceries for me, to just let her know and she would help me out in any way she could. I had never had anyone extend herself to me that way, and I wasn't sure how to respond to it. Don't laugh, but I'm fully admitting to you that in true L.A. fashion, I trashed the cookies because the friendliness was actually odd to me! (Maybe she poisoned the cookies?) But I soon came to realize that kind of familiarity and kindness was typical for Debbie and our neighborhood in general. Debbie ended up being my Bible study leader during my years in Florida and is still a great friend and mentor to me today.

Growing in Faith

One of my first priorities after settling into our new house in Florida was to find a church. Yes, 9/11 had given me a renewed sense of commitment to my faith, but I had already been experiencing a spiritual awakening.

As I mentioned before, I started going to church at the age of twelve and soon thereafter I asked Jesus to be my personal Lord and Savior and I was baptized. I was extremely

excited about what I thought was my new Christian life . . .
but it really didn't end up being any different than my old life.

During my teenage years, I had what one would consider
a very good life. I was on a hit TV show, I was making a lot
of money, and I had a loving and supportive family. I also
had a lot of fans that admired and looked up to me and I was
considered a good role model. I traveled all over the world
meeting people, fans, and other celebrities. But as my life got
busier and busier, church became more of an afterthought.
I'd go when I had time or when I wasn't too busy, but it
wasn't my first priority anymore.

I didn't grow in my Christian walk through my teen
years or even my early twenties. I used God's forgiveness and
grace to live my life the way I wanted. I would knowingly
sin and then pray to God to forgive me for it, just to go back
and commit that same sin all over again. Since my sin wasn't
as "bad" as most other people's sin in my opinion, I figured
I was a pretty good person and it wouldn't bother God if I
sometimes did things that were wrong.

Being a Christian was a label for me. I was a woman, a
daughter, a wife, a Christian. It was one of many things I
was. But what I didn't realize is that unless you're putting
those words into action, they don't mean anything. You can
believe something, but if you're not doing anything about it
or living by it it's just an idea.

Just before we left Canada, Kirk and his wife Chelsea began working on the *Left Behind* movies. I was curious about them, so I started reading the *Left Behind* books and began rethinking my Christian life. I really identified with the character Bruce Barnes. He was a pastor, but he wasn't really a Christian. He was one of the people that was left behind when God took the Christians up to heaven in the rapture. I couldn't understand how a pastor could be left behind. I thought maybe the authors didn't know what they were talking about.

But I started to read the Bible and I came to realize that the *Left Behind* authors were right. I had called myself a Christian for all of those years but I was certainly not living the way God wanted me to. Like Pastor Bruce, I had been using God's forgiveness as a license to live my life the way I wanted to, not the way He wanted me to. I asked myself, "If God came back at this very moment, would I be left behind?" I came to the conclusion that maybe I would.

Shortly after that I talked to Kirk, who asked if he could send me a book by Ray Comfort called *The Way of the Master*. He said it had opened his eyes to something in the Bible he hadn't seen before and he was hoping I might read it too. That book changed my walk with God forever. It talked about the Ten Commandments and showed me my sin in its true light. You see, when I prayed the "sinner's prayer" that day in church when I was twelve, I asked God to forgive my sins, but I didn't even know what my sin was. But God's Law showed me my sin. As I went through every commandment, I saw that I'd broken all of them. Then I learned that God was going to judge me by His standard of goodness, not my own standard or the world's standard. So, while I thought I was a good person compared to other people, I saw that I would never measure up to God's standard.

The Bible says in Acts 17:30–31, "Therefore, having overlooked the times of ignorance, God now commands all people everywhere to repent, because He has set a day when He is going to judge the world in righteousness by the Man He has appointed. He has provided proof of this to everyone by raising Him from the dead" (HCSB). That "Man He has appointed" is Jesus, who lived a sinless life. We will be judged compared to Him, and none of us measures up. He was perfect, and we are not. But He came to earth to live and to die to take the punishment for all of our sins.

It was when I truly recognized and understood my sin and what Jesus did for me that I finally began to follow Him and take my faith seriously. And God has changed me in ways that words can't describe. He has transformed the way I think and live my life. Things that were once important to me no longer have any significance. I know there is nothing more important than my faith. I know that without Christ, the eternal consequences are devastating. And I know that I can always count on Him to guide me.

So after we moved to Florida, I knew God would guide me to a church. Unsurprisingly, He used my brother to do it. I had looked around at a few churches, but I hadn't found the right fit. Then Kirk called and said he had scheduled a speaking engagement at a church in Fort Lauderdale. The event was a year in the future, so he hadn't been there yet, but he had talked to the pastor, Bob Coy, several times and really liked him. He told me to check out Calvary Chapel Fort Lauderdale. It was a thirty-five minute drive from my house, but I took Kirk's advice and went there one Sunday. I loved it. I had found my church home, and there was no question that God had led me there through my brother.

At first, just the kids and I went to church. Val was often either out of town or practicing on Sunday mornings, but once he saw how committed I was to it, he started coming with us when he could. He became a Christian a couple of years later, and to say the least, it was great to be able to have that extra bond between us and really start honoring God together through our marriage and the decisions we were making.

My Ultimate Priority

God is the ultimate priority in my life, and He helps me balance everything else. He is always there in the midst of it all. My relationship with Him colors every aspect of my life. My goal is for all decisions I make and the things I do to be what God would have me do. I don't always succeed, but that's not God's fault. Sometimes it's simply because I misread a situation, need some character building through failure, or simply take my eyes off my rock: God. I find that when I leave Him out of one part of my life, everything gets out of balance. When I allow Him in every part, He will help me keep my life focused and in balance.

I know not everyone agrees with my beliefs or the way I talk about them publicly, but I have experienced what it is like to be changed by God and I can't help but share the Good News with everyone. I know there is nothing more important than faith in Jesus Christ. Without Him, the eternal consequences are devastating and life on earth can't be all that it should be.

If you don't know Jesus, my hope is that you won't wait until the next big tragedy in this country or in your own life in order to take stock of your spiritual life. Instead, I urge you to talk to God right now. Surrender your whole life to Jesus, turn from your sin, and trust in Him with all your heart. Pick up a Bible and start reading. It will change your life, just like it changed mine.

CHAPTER 11

Be True to Your School

Let the wise hear and increase in learning,
and the one who understands obtain guidance.

—PROVERBS 1:5

· · · · · · · · · · · · · ·

As soon as you have kids, you start thinking about their education, right? Wrong! Well, maybe you did, but school wasn't even on my radar during the first few years of Natasha's life. That doesn't mean I don't think education is important; I just didn't realize that many people start planning out their children's education even before they are born.

My dad was always a huge proponent of education. He wanted all four of us kids to get a college education, and that desire didn't change even after Kirk and I became successful in the entertainment industry. Dad wanted us to have something to fall back on if our acting careers suddenly ended. My dad simply desired for us to have as many opportunities as possible. As it turns out, Melissa is the only one of us who has gotten a college degree, but I'm glad Dad wasn't completely disappointed in that area!

Since I don't know what the future holds for my kids, I also want them to get a great education so they can have as many opportunities as possible. They may end up in a career that doesn't require higher education, like their dad and I did, but they may not. Since we don't know God's plans for them, we know that right now a great education is their best bet. We also know that the ability to read well, understand math, and analyze information will serve them well both now and in the future, no matter what they end up doing.

The thing that Val and I have learned when it comes to choosing educational opportunities for our kids is that we need to make the best decision for the family as a whole. The choice has to be a great one for the kids, Val, and me, and it has to work well with our lifestyle at the time. There are more factors involved than just which school has the best academic reputation—it's really a matter of family balance.

I realize that some of you don't have a choice about where your kids go to school. Maybe you and your spouse both have to work full-time to make ends meet and you live in an area where the local public school is the only option. Perhaps you're a single parent and can't afford private education or you don't have time to homeschool. But many of you do have a choice, and regardless of my initial cluelessness about school, I don't think it's a choice to be made lightly. However, I also believe that it's not a choice you have to live with forever. As with most things in life, schooling options can always be open to reevaluation.

The First of Many School Decisions

Once we settled into our new life in Florida, I realized that we needed to send Natasha to preschool. Like I said, I had no idea that people researched schools and compared and contrasted all these different aspects of their educational options. I just thought you sent your kids to the local school and that was it. However, I soon noticed that all the other little kids in the neighborhood went to preschool so I figured it was time to send Natasha to school. Plus, the thought of having a few mornings a week with just two kids instead of all three sounded like a brilliant idea. I checked out a few preschools in the area, but I wasn't impressed with any of them except for one that was located just a couple of blocks from our house. Score! I really liked it when I went for the interview, and we ended up eventually sending all three kids there.

Not too long after Natasha started Pre-K I was sitting in church one Sunday when someone made an announcement about the school that was affiliated with the church. It had been built only a couple of years earlier and was a K-7 school at the time, but they planned to add a grade each year until it was eventually a Pre-K through twelfth grade school. I really hadn't thought much about kindergarten for Natasha. Again, I just kind of figured we'd send her to the closest public school. But I really loved my church and when they were talking about their affiliated school I thought I would mention it to Val.

When I brought it up, I told Val that I realized it sounded a little bit crazy, especially since we lived thirty-five minutes from the school, but I really felt like it was where our kids should go. He wasn't going for it. It was too far away and we didn't need to spend the money for private school. Public school was fine for our kids, and besides, Christian education wasn't important to him anyway.

Val did say he would think about it, but I knew that really meant he wouldn't think about it and would just let time pass. However, during that year we kept going to church and he attended more often and was becoming more open to God and the biblical teachings he was hearing there.

Meanwhile, I kept gently nudging him about the school, and when summer came and we had to make a decision, he said, "Yeah, I think maybe we should look into that school." I was quite surprised and elated about it, and I had no doubt that God had worked on Val's heart about the situation. Not long after, Val and I interviewed with the school and our family was accepted!

While I was super happy that God had worked it out for my kids to go to school at the church I loved so much, it wasn't always easy. After all, it was a thirty-five-minute drive twice a day on school days and at least once on weekends. We could have found a church closer to home and a school just down the road. We could have saved all that time and money. But I knew that it was the best option for my kids and it was where God wanted my children to be—a place where they wouldn't just learn academics, but also learn about Him. Plus, Natasha absolutely loved it, which made it all worth it.

Homeschooling Mama

I would have been happy for all of my kids to spend their entire educational careers at that great school, but God—and the NHL—had other plans. In the spring of 2003, Val was traded to the St. Louis Blues, but with a strange contract clause that said he could be sent back to Florida at the end of the season if the Blues didn't want to sign him. With that uncertainty in mind, we did not move to St. Louis, and Val did rejoin the Panthers for the following season. Then in 2004 Val was again sent packing at the trade deadline, this time to the Dallas Stars. We were yet uncertain about his future because he would be a free agent at the end of the season, so we didn't make the family move to Dallas either.

During the summer of 2004, one of my biggest dreams came true. Val signed a contract with the Los Angeles Kings! I was going home, and my husband was going to get to play in front of my family and friends. You can't even imagine how excited I was to return to my home city. We didn't sell the house in Florida, because Val had only signed a one-year contract. However, we did rent a house in L.A. and we moved the family across the country. This move was a bit less eventful than the tour-bus trip of our prior move.

A hockey season starts in October (with training camp in September) and ends anywhere from April to June, depending on a team's play-off schedule. With this in mind, we weren't sure what to do about school. One option was to move to L.A. early enough so the kids could start school there and then stay until the end of the school year, even if the hockey season ended in April. But we decided we'd rather spend as much time in Florida as we could, so Val suggested I homeschool the kids that year, which wouldn't tie us down to one place for an entire school year. I agreed, because I had quite a few friends from church that home-schooled their kids. I figured if they could do it, I could too. I was familiar with it, I thought it would be manageable, and I really liked the flexibility of the schedule.

That year Natasha was in second grade, Lev was in kindergarten, and Maks was still a toddler. I thought, *How hard can this be? The kids are in second grade and kindergarten. Piece of cake.* I was in for a rude awakening.

Natasha was not on board with the program. She didn't want to work. It would take her hours to do fifteen minutes of work. She would whine, complain, and struggle all day long. I wouldn't let her get up and play until she had done her work, so she would just sit there at the table for five or six hours and not do anything.

Lev, on the other hand, loved it. He quickly discovered that as soon as he got his work done for the day, he could go play. So he cranked out his lessons. I also found out that somehow he had already learned how to read. I hadn't taught him. Val hadn't taught him. But near the beginning of the school year when I told him I was going to read him a book, he said he could read it by himself. I didn't believe him . . . until he took the book from my hands and started reading the story out loud to me. I was shocked! Sure, we had gone over letters and sounds and I knew he could sound out words, but he was able to just read entire sentences without having to sound anything out. He even read with inflection!

So while homeschooling Lev was a dream, homeschooling Natasha made me want to scream. She was so stubborn, and I wanted her to get her work done so I could get the three of them out of our rental house and go somewhere to play. I felt suffocated being in the house all day long. I finally got to the point where I would make any excuse to take them somewhere and use it as a learning experience. After walking to Starbucks, I would have the kids count out the money for our drinks. At the zoo, they would learn about the animals. After a trip to the supermarket, I'd say, "Let's write a summary of our grocery store adventure!" But Natasha still wasn't doing her work.

After a few months of this, Val could see how it wasn't working for Natasha or for me. Let's face it; I wanted to pull my hair out! And if I didn't color it, I'm sure I would have seen some grays. So we both prayed about it and Val told me to go find a school for the kids. I was so relieved. I started looking at schools in the area and found a little Christian elementary school nearby that seemed great. Part of me was sad that the homeschool thing hadn't worked out for us, but overall it was best for the kids and for my own sanity. Natasha obviously needed the social interaction with other kids and the kind of motivation that I couldn't give her. I learned that I'm not the most loving and patient teacher in the world. Lev lessened the blow of me feeling like a failing mom when he told me how much he loved me homeschooling him and that he wanted to continue. But he seemed to understand my reasoning for the new decision and was just as excited to enter a classroom for kindergarten. And as I had suspected, he proved to be a star student!

Meanwhile, to my shock and utter disappointment, Val got badly injured in his first preseason game with the LA Kings. As he picked me up from the Los Angeles International Airport, I remember kissing him an excited hello after coming back from my first mission trip in Ghana, Africa. As we walked to the car, he told me of his injuries and that he needed to have both hip and back surgeries as soon as possible. I couldn't believe I hadn't been there for him and that I had been so far out of the communication loop that he had to wait to tell me until I was home. I suddenly knew how my parents felt on my engagement day!

Because of his extensive surgeries, Val was unable to play or travel with the team that year. That also meant he was at home every day, as I became his full-time nurse, which added to the homeschool pressure and was the final instigator in sending the kids to school. My extended family had all planned on buying season tickets for the Kings, and we were all bummed about not being able to watch Val play in his black and silver colors. It ended up that Val never played another game in the NHL, and I never even got to see him suited up as an LA King. That first preseason game would be the last game of his career. So at the end of the season, we moved back to Florida.

School Hunting . . . Again!

Jumping ahead a little bit, when we ended up moving back to L.A. a couple of years later, we once again had to make a decision about where the kids would go to school. We already had a condo in L.A. that we knew we'd initially move into, so I started researching schools in the surrounding area. I was definitely more comfortable this time around since I was born and raised in L.A. and felt like I had a better handle on what I was looking for in a school. However, I did have high expectations since the school we were leaving was more than I could have wanted as a parent and as a Christian.

We had some friends that had moved back and forth from L.A. to Ft. Lauderdale who also had young children. They told us about the school where their kids had previously attended in the L.A. area which, again, was about a thirty-five-minute drive from where we were living. We checked out that school and also researched a few others. Finally we narrowed it down to three Christian schools and ultimately chose the one our friends had recommended. The school is from Pre-K through eighth grade, so having all three kids in the same school was a total bonus! While I still love our Florida school the most, this school is definitely the best choice for us in L.A.

As a mom, I try to get as involved as I can at school by helping with classroom parties, being a lunch helper, cooking for teacher appreciation days, chaperoning field trips, sitting in on chapel, and participating in community service events. Some years I've been more involved than others, depending on my work schedule, but I always schedule it in and if I have to end up having to cancel I will. But I've learned now that with one child in high school and the other two in middle school, parental help and involvement is becoming less and less, which bums me out. My kids are growing up and becoming more independent. They have to learn to do things on their own, and I'm thankful that Val and I have been so proactive in finding fantastic schools for our kids. I know that a good school will nudge my kids to make decisions for themselves, while allowing them to fail in the process for the sake of maturing. It's my job to take a step to the side but to also never be too far away when they call.

Balancing Choices for Children

Life's about choices and honestly, so is balance. Your time, your money, your relationships, these are all areas where our choices determine our ability to balance that which is most important for a healthy life. If you have children, the decision of how to approach their education is a big decision that will have a huge impact on what your picture of balance turns out to be. I'm going to give you some principles for making educational decisions for your family, but first I want to share something with those of you who may not have children. Let me encourage you to make the lives and education of children part of your life's balance no matter your circumstances.

As I shared earlier, we all have children in our lives—and we all have schools in our communities. If your schedule is flexible, consider volunteering at a school whether you have children or not. And maybe you work during the day, so you can't volunteer at a school, but you could help with an after-school program. Or maybe you'll teach Sunday school at your church. Regardless of the form this takes in your life, children help us see life through a different lens and all children benefit from another adult in their lives who believe in them and make time for them.

Now, for those of you who have children, the specifics of what it looks like for you to invest in the lives of children obviously revolves around those God has given you to love and nurture. And a big part of what that will look like on a day-to-day basis for a big chunk of their lives revolves around how they are schooled. There are so many wonderful choices when it comes to educating your kids. Every parent needs to evaluate their top priorities, which could include academics, religion, sports programs, the arts, social circles, and size. You will need to consider whether your kids—and you—are best suited for public school, private school (either secular or religious), or homeschool. Depending on your family situation, there are likely other factors to think about when choosing a school for your kids.

When contemplating these choices, try not to make sweeping generalizations or assumptions about different forms of schooling. I have many friends and family members who are Christian homeschoolers, but I also know parents with little religious affiliation who homeschool their kids for academic and sports reasons. Private schools aren't necessarily better than public school when you live in a great school district with fantastic teachers. And one pastor friend of mine intentionally put his children in public school so that they could develop their Christian worldview in a secular surrounding.

No one type of schooling is "right" for all families or all kids. Each parent knows his or her child's strengths and weaknesses. My kids are very different when it comes to personalities and learning abilities. What's right for Lev isn't necessarily right for Maks, and Natasha's high school won't necessarily be the right choice for the boys. Everyone has a different and unique situation. It's best to understand your circumstances and make a decision that is best for your family, not what's most popular with your extended family, friends, or the proverbial Joneses. It's up to each individual family to decide where God wants them to be and to determine which school will best help their kids become the kind of people they want them to grow up to be.

CHAPTER 12

California Dreamin'

But seek first the kingdom of God and his righteousness,
and all these things will be added to you.
—Matthew 6:33

• • • • • • • • • • • •

I like to joke around and say that when Val doesn't
really want to do something I've suggested to him,
he'll say, "I'll pray about it," which is just his way of
saying he doesn't want to do it. It's kind of the Christian take
on a parent saying to a kid, "I'll think about it." You know it's
just not going to happen.

But the truth is, even though Val uses that as an avoid-
ance mechanism, he and I really do pray about things before
we do them (or don't do them, as the case might be). You
know by now that I don't make huge life decisions alone. In

fact, any decisions that have any sort of impact on my life, my family, or those around me are made in conjunction with my husband and, most important, with God. The Bible says we are to seek *Him* first—not our feelings, not the world, not our peers, not logic. I'll be the first to admit that I don't always do what He says or what I know is right, but I do know that He will give me the best guidance, whether I decide to take it or not.

When it comes to major life events, you know how excited I was when we moved to Florida. I was ready for fun and sun, baby! But that excitement was nothing compared to when we actually moved back "home" to California for the long term. Though moving was a decision that gave me much joy, it wasn't one that was made lightly. That choice to change not only our location, but also our lifestyle, was made after much, much prayer and consideration.

Two Coasts

After Val retired from the NHL, we settled back down in our house in Florida. Since he was no longer working, a year later we prayerfully made the decision that I would open up the door to start working again. We talked about a possible move back to Los Angeles if I was offered consistent work on a TV show. Val said he was willing to do it if it made sense for our family.

The Bible says, "Commit your way to the LORD; trust in him, and he will act" (Ps. 37:5), so that's what we did. Val and I knew that even though we might have our own plans of what we wanted to happen, we needed to leave it up to God and put it into His hands. Though it's sometimes hard to let go, I've learned over the years that when I give up my hold on my own dreams and desires and instead trust God with them, He will come through in ways that I never could have imagined. This specific time in my life was no exception.

A few months after my managers put my name back on the radar and started looking for work for me, they called me. "ABC Family called and they want to offer you a part on a new series that's been picked up about gymnastics. They have an idea for the character, playing the girlfriend to one of the gymnasts' dad. They're open to talking to you about the character and want to have a meeting." Cue the squeals from my end of the phone line. There's always something about a job offer that seems surreal to me. I always want to ask, "Are you *sure* they asked for *me?*" My dad has always been cynical about the entertainment business, and it must have rubbed off on me. After more than thirty years, he still can't believe I'm employed by "Hollywood," which he always claims is fairy-tale land. He's kind of right. And you never know with this business, which is why I still freak out with excitement when I get a call.

So I watched the pilot, which had already been filmed, and I flew to L.A. for the initial meeting at ABC Family and the *Make It or Break It* show producers. The meeting went well and I was excited to play a character that was a bit of an enigma. The audience wouldn't initially be able to figure out if she had a true and honest heart for her boyfriend Steve Tanner (ironic name, I know), or if she was just another gold digger looking to cash in. They would play the relationship off of Steve's daughter Lauren, and the audience wouldn't know my yet-unnamed character's motives until about half-way through the first season. I loved the idea, and I thought the possible double-minded character would be really fun to play.

Before Val and I made a decision about whether or not I would take the job, we had several things to consider about the job itself. Was it a good project? Was the show something I wanted to be a part of for the long term? Did any red flags arise in the initial meetings, script, and story lines? What are my personal boundaries as an actor, and is the show willing to accept them?

All of those answers were acceptable, so the next set of questions was about our family. What would my day-to-day schedule look like? How many hours a day and days a week would I be working? How many months of work would each season consist of? Is the family on board for moving back to L.A.? Where would the kids go to school? How would we manage our new lifestyle? Would the move be worth it financially? Could we make the move without going into debt? Once we broke everything down and prayed about it, we realized that we could make it all work.

After the deal was done and the contracts were signed, I got a call that the character's name would be Summer Van Horne . . . and she would be a Christian. I was elated! The producers said that after getting to know me at our meeting, and because of a few boundaries that I expressed, they thought making Summer a Christian would add depth and a different point of view to the show's colorful cast. It ended up that Summer wasn't in the relationship with Steve for the money, and that story line didn't really end up being a big part of the show. Instead, she was instantly a positive influence, a mentor, and a listening ear to Lauren, the bad girl of the show. I loved every minute of playing Summer and she'll always have a piece of my heart.

Remember what I said earlier about what God can do when we let Him? I could never have dreamed up a better role for my reentry into the entertainment industry than that of Summer Van Horne. I can only attribute it to God's control over all things and His protection of me as I came back on the TV scene. To this day, I continue to thank Him for that and many other amazing works He has done in my life. I can think of no better words than this prayer from Ephesians 3:20–21: "Now to Him who is able to do above and beyond all that we ask or think according to the power that works in us—to Him be glory in the church and in Christ Jesus to all generations, forever and ever. Amen" (HCSB).

Responsibilities of a Role Model

I mentioned that I have boundaries as an actor, as most actors do. I can say without hesitation that I won't do gratuitous nudity or sex scenes, but my boundaries get much more detailed than that. They change over time, just like priorities often do. When you're in different stages of life, your priorities can change based on your responsibilities and what your life looks like at the time. With new seasons in life, you change your parameters and way of looking at things. Likewise, my boundaries as an actor have changed based on my season of life, my commitment to my Christian faith, and my level and areas of influence.

For instance, I never thought about how a "mom" role could influence my viewers until I had children of my own. Also, before living for Christ, I didn't pay much attention to how some scripts could be dishonoring to God. There are certainly days when I'm watching a movie and for a second I wish I didn't have such strong convictions about the roles I take and could delve into a character that is uncharacteristically me. Don't get me wrong; my boundaries don't mean I can't take on a role of a person who is completely different than me, but they definitely limit my roles and the projects I'm willing to do.

Even though it's a challenge to be a Christian in Hollywood when I'm surrounded by so much that is counter to everything I believe in, I look at it as an opportunity to be light in a dark place. Whether you're conservative or liberal, Christian or atheist, or anything in between, you'll likely agree that there is much that is not good in Hollywood. But I believe that it's possible to maintain Christian integrity in the entertainment industry, and there are plenty of people to prove that, including my brother. I keep myself focused and on the right path by keeping my priorities in line when it comes to my faith. Every day I try my best to spend time in prayer and in God's Word. Going to church and small group Bible study each week is always a top priority and those two days are my favorite days of the week. But admittedly, due to my kids' sports commitments, we sometimes have to supplement a sermon at home. It's a little more challenging when I'm working on location somewhere because I don't always have a car or the routine and familiar locations of home, but really, I just need my Bible and a quiet space in order to spend time with God.

Since I was ten years old I've been told I'm a role model. Whether or not it was true, I believed it then and I still do. I see myself as a role model not only as an actor, but also as a mom, a wife, a friend, a sister, a daughter, and a Christian. Even at a young age I would consider the effects of my decisions on those who looked up to me. However, I never considered it to be a burden; it was a responsibility and one that I felt accountable to and comfortable with. Thankfully I didn't have the desire—like many child actors and entertainers do—to reinvent myself in early adulthood as someone completely different than my childhood persona. I didn't want to emerge in a new light, because a new light would have been a dark one, and there was nothing in my soul that wanted to be a part of that.

I am so grateful for the influence God gave me through my *MIOBI* character, Summer, and the role model she was to not only the characters on the show, but also to young viewers. Two issues she was very adamant about were sexual purity and her ultimate faith in God. This was annoying to some viewers, as can be expected. There's never going to be a character that every viewer completely identifies with or agrees with on any issue. But I received countless e-mails from people who were grateful to watch a character who had positive moral values that went against the grain of typical Hollywood fare. In most shows and movies, anyone with a Christian influence is more likely portrayed as a hypocrite. They say one thing and do another when "nobody" is looking. But Summer was firm in her convictions. She did struggle and make a few questionable decisions along the way when it came to the men she dated, but that just made her more real, because we all waver and make mistakes at times. But overall, her heart was in the right place and she always wanted to do the right thing. For a fictional character, she was a woman who had her priorities straight.

Let the Circus Begin

Moving back to L.A. and going back into the entertainment industry meant I had to reevaluate and restructure things in order to balance it all. Not only did I still have God, family, friendships, and everything else that had been in my life, but now I had to figure out how to throw work into the mix. I knew work would definitely not usurp the place of God or family, but how exactly would it fit into my life? After all, I would have to leave my kids at home while I went to work. That didn't mean it was more important than my kids, but I would definitely need to learn to balance this "new" part of my life with everything else.

When it comes down to it, balancing life is never easy and nobody is going to do it perfectly every single day. We all need to realize that it's just not possible. Balancing it all is about prioritizing and reevaluating each day's priorities. There are some things that are important every day—like God and family—and others that aren't always as important, like work. And in reality, God and family will overlap with pretty much everything we do in a day. There are some days when I have to focus most of my energy on my work, and that's okay because my other priorities are a part of why I work. I have a job to help support my family. I work as a way to be a godly influence in the lives of the people who watch the projects I'm a part of or who come to the Christian women's conferences where I speak.

It can be difficult to juggle all the parts of my life at times, especially when I have to be on the road for a movie shoot or a conference. But Val places just as much of an importance on family as I do, so whether I'm working in town or not, Val and I work with each other's schedules to make sure one of us is always at home with the kids. We certainly ask family members, friends, and babysitters to help out when it's necessary. Val and I are two people with three kids, and we just can't ever be more than two places at once!

And of course, every so often we realize that our lives have gotten too crazy and something has to give. When that's the case, it's always work that takes the backseat for me. Missing out on a job would be a short-term regret, but reducing the priority of my kids for long periods of time would be a life-long regret for me.

I have found that when Val and I have our overarching priorities firmly set, we can easily make the right decision when it's crunch time and we have to decide what has to go, which area will suffer, or what we'll pass up. When I know what has the most value and eternal importance—faith and family—and I make decisions based on that conviction, I don't have to feel guilty or feel like I've failed when I do have to say no or give something up. There is a sense of relief that comes when I realize I said no because it wasn't important enough in the first place, at least at that moment in time. Just recently I had to make the decision to cut back in one area of my life—my online magazine.

In November 2011 I launched an online magazine called *RooMag*. It came about because I wanted to create an online community where women could support, encourage, and trade secrets with each other so that together we could be one of the most powerful influences on the future of our world. I realized that modern women in the trenches of life and motherhood can feel isolated at times and be in need of a watering hole where they can gather with like-minded women and seek fulfillment and purpose in who they are. So, along with over twenty other contributors, I began to produce inspiring, encouraging, and how-to articles to daily motivate wives, singles ladies, and moms alike.

While I've loved every aspect of my RooMag ministry, in early 2013 I realized that I once again needed to reevaluate my priorities and that there wasn't enough room for Roo to continue in the same manner. The decision was made more difficult because I truly believed God had initially steered me in this direction, but I realized I couldn't work at it the way I intended to while keeping everything else in my life balanced. While Roo ministered to thousands of women, my ministry at home was suffering. So once again, I had to make the decision to either forge ahead, causing something more important to suffer, or to close up my investment and scrap the time and energy I had expended so diligently. So I made the decision to transfer Roo and my blog over to my personal website and manage it on a much smaller level until God showed me something different.

Accepting God's Grace in Failure

After reading so far you may think I either have it all figured out all the time or I'm a huge imposter. I'm actually neither one. I do strive to keep my priorities straight and keep my life and my family members' lives in balance and much of the time God gives me the strength, wisdom, and grace to do so, but there are times when my focus goes off Him and I experience my share of failure. The trick is to trust in God to bring me back to where I need to be.

I'm going to end this chapter by being very transparent and giving you a little glimpse into one of my journal entries. I can look back now and chuckle at the intensity of my feelings, because I was in a pretty low spot and was physically sick on top of it. But I was being truly honest with myself, even though not all of my thoughts were true.

> *January 21, 2011*
> *I'm in Santa Fe filming* Truth Be Told *and I've never been more physically sick. I'm nauseous, dehydrated, over-medicated, stressed out, feeling the pressure, tired, homesick, and above all, spiritually dry. Dry probably isn't the right word. Empty? Abandoned? And no, God hasn't abandoned me. I've abandoned Him.*
>
> *I'm not the person I want to be. I'm so overwhelmed with my life that it's killing me. I feel like I'm on a high-speed train taking me to wonderland, except all I want to do is get off. And I can't! It's moving too fast. And what if I jump? Will I*

break? Will I ever catch another train again? I know the answer but I'm too afraid to leap.

I never intended to work this much. I never intended to be away from my kids this much. MIOBI's schedule increased, the book has been released, and a wonderful movie has been offered. It's everything I've been hoping for. And yet God convicted me of something I shouldn't do and I did it anyway. I don't know if I'm really sick or just sick of myself and my decisions. I feel like a failure.

I talk about being the best wife and mom I can be. I say work should be third place, but clearly it has become number one. It's not that I even want it to be, but I can't stop it. I don't know how to say no. I've wanted to return to acting and a career for more than ten years and it's finally here, but I can't enjoy it the way I was hoping to. That's what's so hard. I love being on set and acting and being an author. I love being one of those Hollywood moms who seems to have it all together, and it's killing me that I seem to! I actually take pride in being humble. And after examining myself these past few months, I'm anything but humble. I'm full of pride and self-absorption. I don't love the Lord the way I want to or have professed during the past year.

I'm so weak. I'm out of control. I can't balance a thing. Who am I kidding? Who am I fooling? Everyone but God, apparently.

Today has been awful, yet I've read the first chapter of Nancy Leigh DeMoss's book Brokenness, *and I think that is where God is trying to bring me. I think I'm so worn out my body has failed because God is trying to get hold of my heart. Break me, break me, break me. I want to be undone. I want to do what is right. I want to feel so low I can only look up. I don't want to live in this state of mind anymore. I think I'm hopeless, but Lord, I don't want to be!*

Things have slowed down for me since this journal entry. I've reconnected and am back in the place I want to be. I just took some time to get there. I believe we all need to learn to give ourselves grace each day and take a deep breath, especially when we just can't do it all. I'm still learning to accept God's grace on a daily basis and recognize the pressure of high expectations I put on myself. I don't always keep it all balanced, and I have my moments of self-doubt. But ultimately I know I can do all things through Christ who breaks and then strengthens me.

CHAPTER 13

For Better or for Worse

Therefore a man shall leave his father and his mother and hold fast to his wife, and they shall become one flesh.
—Genesis 2:24

. . . .

I want you take a moment to stick your finger in this page, close the book, and look at the front cover. What do you think? Can you relate to that picture? I totally felt like I was in an episode of *I Love Lucy* when we took that photo, and for good reason . . . because my life often seems like a comedy of errors! I may have been hamming it up for the camera, but life sure can get a bit overwhelming. There are so many things going on at once that it's no wonder sometimes I'm not quite sure what's happening. What I've realized is that when things get too crazy in my life, the first thing to suffer is often my relationship with Val.

Once you have kids, marriage can easily be the first thing that goes out the window. It's easy (relatively!) when it's just the two of you, but once you throw in some crying babies, hectic job schedules, and eventually some rebellious teenagers, things definitely change. You become a full-time taxi driver, chef, housekeeper, tutor, stylist, craft expert, errand runner, and anything else that your family needs you to be. Not only that, but with each growing child, the needs of your family change, and you have less and less free time. *And* on top of that, you are supposed to amicably agree about everything with your spouse!

That can definitely cause tension or put a distance between you that you swore would never happen. This has happened to Val and me, without a doubt. After seventeen years, it's bound to! But I've learned that we have to make a conscious effort to keep things going and moving forward, together, in a positive direction.

Changing Gears

During all the years of having a relatively predictable lifestyle while Val was playing hockey and I was staying home with the kids, we figured out how to keep our marriage on a pretty even keel. But that all changed once Val retired from hockey, I started working again, and we moved to L.A. Once again, everything in our lives changed, and our marriage needed to change with it.

Val made the transition out of hockey very well. Many times professional athletes struggle with the change of lifestyle. They spend their whole lives preparing for and then competing in a strenuous, high-profile, elite career, only to have that career end before they're forty years old. It's understandable that most people would have a difficult transition. But I think the key for Val was that he already had his second career in mind and was starting to put it in place. He was eager to start his new job as proprietor of a wine label.

Early on in Val's childhood in the Soviet Union, food wasn't always readily available. Times were tough, and his parents did their best to feed their children, but there wasn't always enough to go around. So when Val came to North America at age seventeen to start his professional hockey career in Montreal, he dove straight into the mecca of fine dining and became an instant foodie. With great food often comes great wine, and many of Val's veteran teammates showed him how to pair them together. Val started learning the nuances of wine and he grew an appreciation, passion, and love for it. He knew that when he retired from hockey, he wanted to go into the food and wine business by opening a restaurant and/or having his own wine label.

A few years before Val retired from hockey, we went on our first trip to Napa Valley, and I have to tell you it rivals Tuscany any day of the year. We fell in love with the gorgeous scenery and the wine, and Val started making connections to learn the trade, farming skills, and business of making wine. By the time he hung up his skates for good, he was all set for his second career. Bure Family Wines was born.

I'm very grateful that Val was on top of making sure his transition from hockey to his new passion of the wine label went smoothly. I know many ex-hockey wives who have to kick their husbands out of the house just to get them to go do something, because they're not used to having them home so much. But I didn't need to help with Val's shift except to support his new dream. I've always been his biggest cheerleader and I'll never stop shouting from the sidelines. (Our wine is the best, by the way!)

Focusing on the Family

If you're at all familiar with California geography, you will have realized that Los Angeles is really nowhere near Napa Valley. During certain seasons throughout the year,

Val travels up to Napa every week. So how do we make that work? Well, it can get a little crazy at times, especially since Val coaches both boys' hockey teams. It's really not so crazy for me, though, because much of the time it's no different than when he was playing hockey and was on the road for days at a time. In fact, when I'm not working, it's actually a little easier because the kids are older.

The hardest part is making sure I'm able to be in three places at once. I've invented this handy machine . . . just kidding. I wish I could, though! And don't we all. Now *that* would be a good way to balance it all. The kids' schedules are challenging for sure, especially on days when the boys have to be at the hockey rink and Natasha has to be at play practice or a tennis lesson. My kids aren't driving yet (one more year!), so finding neighbors for carpool is a must. Sometimes I hire a sitter to do some ferrying if Val or I are out of town, but most of the time we manage it, though I really don't know how. L.A. is very spread out and it takes forever to get anywhere, so when you're trying to get three kids to three different places it can definitely be a challenge.

But when Val is home, he's literally at home. He does the majority of the cooking, he drives the kids to school and their various practices, he coaches hockey, and he just genuinely likes being at home with his family. Aside from golfing with his buddies and working out, he doesn't fill his time with much besides being with the kids and me in the afternoons and evenings. He even got rid of his iPhone awhile back because he found himself looking at it too much and felt it was a distraction. He shrugs his shoulders in a couldn't-care-less attitude when friends poke fun at him for having an old flip phone. But he just says, "Why should everyone have my attention immediately? Are they more important than my family when I'm sitting down to dinner or playing a board game with my kids?" He even made the decision to only answer e-mails during a set time of the day.

I admire Val's ability to cut out those distractions so he can focus on his family. That's serious discipline, and it's not something I'm quite ready for to that extent, to tell you the truth. Val definitely sets the tone for family priority in our home, and the kids know it. That helps keep our family balanced.

Quality Time

Though Val and I do love spending time with the family as a whole, we also love to spend quality time with just each other. However, we have differing opinions on how that time should best be spent. I love spending short amounts of time together on a frequent basis, while Val likes weekends away without the kids.

I enjoy having lunch with Val, going on a few errands together, taking a walk or a jog, or going on a dinner date every week or two. This allows me to share the day-to-day stuff with him—my emotions, concerns, excitement, business opportunities, or anything else that is important to me. I'm a woman, I'm a talker, and I like connecting frequently.

Val would prefer to whisk me away on a trip without the kids. He prefers connecting one-on-one away from home, without the distractions of everyday life. This helps him recharge, get reacquainted with me and himself, and come back with a new sense of self and a fresh set of eyes.

Both methods are great, but without recognizing that both are equally important to our relationship, doing only one or the other would never satisfy our marriage. We've learned this the hard way over many hours of discussion, and not without tears. Sometimes we still need reminding, and when we finally figure it out, it's like an "ah-ha" moment. We both know these things about each other, so how did we miss it?

So we go for walks, on dinner dates, to the post office, on one- or two-day trips to Napa, and any other getaways we can manage when the opportunity arises. We're often invited to charity events around the country, and we sometimes have business trips that we turn into a quick romantic getaway if possible. But don't let me fool you into thinking those quick trips are easy for us to go on. They're not, just like I'm sure getting out of town isn't easy for you. With our kids' crazy schedules, we have to set up carpools, sleepovers, and so on before we can head out on our own, and sometimes it's just not worth it if there's too much going on with the kids. But if it's remotely possible, we make it happen, because we know it will not only help our relationship as husband and wife, but it will also help us come back as better parents.

3 Keys to a Healthy Marriage

A healthy marriage is a marriage with sex. Just because I'm a Christian, doesn't mean I can't talk about sex, you know! On the contrary, as a married couple, this is one of the most important details of our marriage. If the sexual intimacy isn't there, I can guarantee the relationship isn't there in any other form. Sex needs to be high on the priority list for a balanced marriage. I won't go into detail, because there are plenty of marriage books out there, but when the physical relationship is lacking, so is everything else. I know from experience that it just makes everything that much more agreeable.

Another key for our marriage is that Val and I regard each other as higher than ourselves. In other words, I have to put Val on a pedestal and treat him like royalty, even if he doesn't always deserve it. And he doesn't, trust me (just as I don't always deserve the love and respect with which he treats me). But I listen to Val and he listens to me. We don't always get it right, but we try to pay attention to the details. What are his likes and dislikes? What's important to him that might not be important to me? Do I still honor him by doing those things or putting an importance on them? Do I smile at him and make an effort to kiss him each morning and evening? Do I tell him I love him often? How *should* I tell him—or show him—I love and respect him?

Each person's love language is different, and it helps immensely to know what your spouse's love language is. If you're not familiar with what I'm talking about, I highly recommend the book *The Five Love Languages* by Gary Chapman. It's a wonderful tool in helping decode what makes your spouse (and children) feel most loved. Just don't be surprised if your spouse's love language is totally different from yours.

The final key for a healthy marriage is prayer. In fact, I believe prayer is the most important way to keep a marriage balanced. I pray for Val every day. I really do. I pray for him specifically in ways I'd love to see God work in his life. And no, I don't pray that God changes him to be the way I want him to be, but I pray that he will grow and become more mature in the qualities and characteristics that God has already given him. I want him to become more and more the man that God intended him to be, just like I want to become more and more the woman that God has intended me to be.

Each day I pray for a strengthened marriage and for a wonderful physical intimacy. I ask God to give us a union that will stand the test of time, that with each trial we face it would only strengthen our already tight bond. I pray that our love will continue to grow together as we grow as people. I pray that Val will have a compassionate heart for others, that he will have a constant thirst for God, and that he will be a strong spiritual leader for our family. To me, nothing is sexier than a man who honors God. There are many other things that I pray for, and when I write a book about prayer someday I'll tell you all about them.

A Biblical Marriage

If your marriage is not where you would like it to be, I encourage you to try some of the principles I just described. And you know what? I didn't make them up. They came straight from the Bible.

Yes, the Bible tells married people to have sex . . . and lots of it. First Corinthians 7:3–5 says, "A husband should fulfill his marital responsibility to his wife, and likewise a wife to her husband. A wife does not have the right over her own body, but her husband does. In the same way, a husband does not have the right over his own body, but his wife does. Do not deprive one another sexually—except when you agree for a time, to devote yourselves to prayer. Then come together again; otherwise, Satan may tempt you because of your lack of self-control" (HCSB). Sex in marriage is good, my friends! In fact, it is commanded.

God's Word also has much to say about putting others' needs and desires before your own. Philippians 2:3 says, "Do nothing from selfish ambition or conceit, but in humility count others more significant than yourselves." I love that this verse tells it like it is. God knows that we're all tempted to be selfish and conceited and that we want *our* needs to be met. But we actually find that we will be more fulfilled and blessed when we put someone else's needs before our own. We often do this for our kids, but it's imperative that we also do it with our spouses.

It comes as no surprise that the Bible tells us to pray. In fact, 1 Thessalonians 5:17 commands us to "pray without ceasing." What? How is that possible? I don't think it means we have to pray every single minute of every day, but that we should make a habit of prayer. Make a practice of praying for your spouse. You can't imagine what might happen when you do.

I truly attribute the strength of my marriage to the Lord. Val and I strive to live our lives according to what God's Word has to say about marriage. We find that when we live by those principles, our relationship just works. We still disagree sometimes and have our problems, but when conflicts arise, we resolve them by going to the Bible. We approach things biblically so that God will be pleased with each of us and with our marriage. It's all about us being the people God wants us to be individually and as a couple.

CHAPTER 14

Smells Like Teen Spirit

These words that I am giving you today are to be in your heart. Repeat them to your children. Talk about them when you sit in your house and when you walk along the road, when you lie down and when you get up.
—Deuteronomy 6:6–7 (HCSB)

• • • • • • • • • • • • • •

Not long ago, Natasha had a Socratic seminar question in theology class about whether or not certain things were sins. The issues they debated included things such as abortion, lying, pride, eating fast food, getting tattoos, and suicide. Natasha and I agreed on all but three of the thirty issues. While discussing one of the actions on which we had disagreed, Natasha responded with a line of thinking that was based on biblical teaching.

She took broad biblical principles and then applied them to a situation. I realized that she wasn't being driven by emotion, she was drawing conclusions based upon what she had been taught at home and church about what the Bible says. Even though she had drawn a different conclusion about the application of that principle than I had, I was thrilled because of how she came to the conclusion.

I use this as a demonstration to say: *They're listening to you!* I was so proud of my daughter for forming her opinion about one of life's big questions from a biblical perspective, and I knew then that not everything I say goes in one ear and out the other despite her regular fingers-in-ears, "Lalala, I'm not listening to you" attitude.

Do you ever feel like your kids don't learn anything from what you say or try to teach them? I do, on a daily basis! Proverbs 1:8 says, "Listen, my son, to your father's instruction, and don't reject your mother's teaching" (HCSB). I think this is fantastic advice, but I often feel like my kids are not on the same page as the writer of Proverbs. However, that doesn't mean I shouldn't strive to keep teaching my kids. If God wants my kids to listen to and learn from their parents, that means we need to keep instructing them, no matter what. I think God helps me along with that by occasionally reminding me that they are listening and—more important—learning. And sometimes I even learn from them, as the story above illustrates.

As I write this, I have two teenage kids and one preteen. Being the mother to two teenagers (one of whom is a *girl*) is one of the most difficult things I have experienced in my life. We all know how much things change from generation to generation. Today's world is very different than it was when I was growing up in the 1980s and early '90s, mostly due to technology. Some things stay the same—like teenage girl drama—but everything is so much more public, immediate, and easily accessible these days. It's hard to know how to handle it all.

I have very similar desires for my kids that my parents had for me. I want them to be good, upstanding citizens. I want them to be kind and compassionate. I want them to put others' needs before their own. And I want them to love and serve God. Are they going to learn those things on their own? To some extent, possibly, but for the most part, Val and I need to teach them both by word and by example. We also need to establish rules and boundaries both to keep them safe and to teach them to live godly lives.

Boundaries of Love

In my family, boundaries are the name of the game when it comes to guiding my kids along the right path. My parents set them for me as a teenager, and I definitely set them for my own kids. I find that as my kids get older I have to be more creative in how I discipline them and love them. No teenager likes it when you set limits for them, but we have to do it because we love them.

I know my kids would agree with me that I'm a tough mom, because they've told me so. While I don't think I'm the toughest out there (they never know how good they've got it!), I hope I balance that toughness with plenty of love and affection. The rules and boundaries Val and I have put into place are there for our kids' best interests. I see them as a sign of love, even though teenagers—and even some parents—might not view them that way at all. If I want my kids to learn how to live balanced lives, I need to set limits and parameters in place to help them. If kids didn't have rules, most of them would undoubtedly live out-of-control lives—subsisting on junk food, spending their days sitting on the couch playing video games or staring at the computer, and having no respect for parents, teachers, bosses, government, and all other authority figures. In my mind, boundaries are the foundation for love and balance.

So in which areas of our kids' lives do Val and I set boundaries? All of them! Sure, the lines move as the kids get older. Their needs and desires and propensities all evolve over the years, and our parenting techniques and the rules we set must change with them, though that's not always easy. Plus, having kids with three very different personalities makes it even harder because there's no one formula that works for all of them. Different approaches work for each child, so we have to find the right methods that each of them will respond to. That's definitely challenging, but as parents we must always be up for a challenge! If you go into parenting prepared, knowing that certain stages will be especially taxing, then you won't be surprised when they arise. You'll have on your armor and will be ready to go!

One of the areas in which twenty-first-century parents nearly always have trouble with setting parameters is with technology and social media. Since we didn't have much more than a portable CD player, Super Mario Bros., MTV, great family shows like *The Cosby Show* and reruns of *Happy Days*, and possibly a personal phone line in our bedrooms, we can't really look at our parents' example to try to figure out how to deal with our own kids when it comes to smart phones, tablet computers, computer use, the Internet, risqué TV shows on 800+ channels, and much, much more. In our house, we seem to be constantly modifying our boundaries concerning these issues as the kids get older and the technology changes.

I don't have any secret info to share that addresses or solves all of these issues in an instant, but like any mom, I read up on the latest books, talk with other like-minded parents to hear their views, and sit in on parenting conferences at my children's schools about technology use, drug use, and sexual integrity. I also look for trusted family resources and conferences in my area that are geared towards teens on these subjects.

A few of our family rules have been: the kids can get a cell phone—not a smart phone—at age thirteen and can sign up for social media profiles on sites like Facebook, Keek, and Instagram. Lev did get an account a few months before turning thirteen, which I allowed because his maturity level was different than Natasha's at the time. Also, I limit the amount of profiles they have on social networking sites, and Twitter isn't an option. That's not because it's bad, but because I don't see the point for a child. I monitor their pages as well as having full access to them. If there is inappropriate content or language after three warnings, or I discover they're keeping secrets from me, the account gets deleted. Natasha's photo rules include no puckered lips or posed bathing suit pictures. Remember, we live at the beach, which means this is a constant concern as so many of her friends post photos with each other in their bikinis, even though most of them are just being playful, not intentionally sexy. I'm also an online "friend" with as many of my kids' friends as will accept me. This helps me form a better opinion of the people my kids want to hang out with and what those kids are like outside of parental supervision. This is one of those areas where balance is guided by boundaries, which is all informed by knowledge. We have to understand the temptations as well as what our kids' friends are like in order to set appropriate boundaries and balance.

I also monitor the kids' music (no explicit versions allowed) and have privacy settings on all our TVs. Only Val and I have the passcode for any shows rated PG-13 and over. We want to instill positive and godly values in our kids at a young age, so that they will be able to make good decisions as they grow and mature. That means we need to have a balance between rules and trust. As the kids get older the balance will tip more toward the trust side . . . that's the goal, anyway!

Val and I also have boundaries when it comes to our kids' health. We've been teaching them how to treat their bodies well by eating wholesome and nutritious foods and exercising. There are foods we do not buy or allow the kids to eat (at least on a regular basis), and we expect them to be physically active either by participating in sports or by jogging or working out. As I've said before, we know that the healthier our kids are, the more opportunities they'll have to do the things they want to do as they get older. It's also another way to teach commitment and discipline within ourselves. Val and I do our best to model that for them in our lives too.

We have more rules when it comes to friends and sleepovers, the clothes they wear, and their hygiene. They need to learn to fulfill their roles as students with homework and studies. They also must fulfill home obligations with chores such as keeping their rooms and bathrooms clean, doing laundry, helping cook meals, taking out the trash, doing dishes, and walking and feeding the dog. Val and I have also put boundaries in place regarding attitudes, talking or acting disrespectfully, and lying.

What do we do when one of the kids challenges a boundary or steps over the line? In a nutshell, we discipline them. When they were young, we would give them a spank on the bottom with instruction in love and prayer. As they have gotten older, we take away items or privileges like phones, TV time, computer time, or hang-out time with friends. Recently, we couldn't seem to find anything that was effective for Natasha, so I did what any mother of a fifteen-year-old girl would do. I took away all her clothes, shoes, and accessories and left her with one pair of tennis shoes, one pair of jeans, one pair of workout shorts, two T-shirts, underwear, socks, and one set of pajamas. I dropped off three extra-large garbage bags full of clothes, shoes, and jewelry at my neighbor's house so she could store them until Natasha earned her stuff back. It took a few months, but she did! There are plenty of books out there to help you find creative ways to discipline your children, so do a little research if you're struggling.

Val and I strike a good balance in discipline. There's no good cop/bad cop in our house. Both of us are disciplinarians, but we are also loving and gentle. If the kids disobey me when Val's not home, I don't wait for him to come home to discipline them. The same goes for Val. While I am slightly more lenient than he is, we are both on the same page. Since we operate in this way, the kids know they can't manipulate us, although they don't stop trying! We are a united front.

I Choose to Fight

As you can tell, I am a big proponent of being a proactive parent. I think it's vitally important for us to teach and guide our children in all areas of life. However, I don't always do the best job at this. Can you relate? It's easy to slowly let things slide, and then eventually you realize you've totally failed your kids, without even realizing it. I wrote a blog post on my friend Ruth Schwennk's website "The Better Mom" titled, "I Choose to Fight" (August 7, 2012). This was written at a time when I knew I had totally let my kids down.

I am failing my family. That sounds dramatic, and it is. There is no catch—no secondary line to soften it up and make light of it.

I am failing my children.

I've been doing what I thought was my best to raise my kids in a Christian home despite not being raised in one myself. My husband is a believer of eight years, but he is still trying to find himself as our spiritual leader. I try my best to be the example to them as a woman, wife, mother, and role model, effortlessly falling short in some way every day while letting life get the better of me and my self-control.

Here's where I've ended up. I used to read my kids Bible stories every night. I used to make games out of memorizing Scripture. I used to test them on Bible facts over dinner, giving them prizes if they got the answers right. I used to dance around the house singing worship songs and inviting them to play along with me. I used to buy them a Bible study and devotional each year in hopes of them spending time with the Lord each morning on their own. I used to go over their questions and answers with them when they did. I used to pray individually with them each night before bed. And somehow, as my kids became preteens and teenagers, I've slacked.

Attitudes seem to be the norm at this age, but the disrespect and disobedience shouldn't be . . . not if my kids know Christ. I don't expect perfection and do expect mistakes, but what I don't understand is the lack of humility and remorse. No, not by the way I've raised them, not by the things I've taught them for the last thirteen-plus years. Sure, there are always glimpses of goodness, but they seem to be getting farther and fewer as time goes on. Since when did my child become "that kid"?

My heart aches, my heart cries, my heart screams out, "Why? Where did I go wrong? Why isn't this working out the way I thought it would? What's the deal?"

The deal . . . is me.

When did I stop reading the Bible to my kids? When did I stop encouraging them along in their faith? When did I think their Christian school would be the influence? When did I let youth group become the teacher? When did I think that by letting them see me do my Bible study every day it would be enough and not have to do one with them? When did I stop getting involved because I hoped they would take the lead on their own?

There's never been an easy time to raise children or teenagers. With each decade comes new challenges that grandparents didn't experience with their kids. Times are always changing, but God's Word doesn't. New solutions will arise, but God's Word always stays the same.

I must be a teacher in my home. I must help my children read the Word of God every day. How else will they know it? If they haven't developed their own relationship with Christ at this point, it's only going to get weaker as they get older. I mistook giving them independence for letting go of my responsibilities. The cycle stops here.

Praise be to God for showing me my failure. Praise be to God for giving me grace. Praise be to God for giving me the tools to raise godly children. It's all in the Bible. We have to read it. We have to discuss it. We have to apply it. We have to live it . . . *daily*.

You learn a new habit by repeating it day after day. How will my kids know God if I'm not teaching them every single day? There are no excuses. There is not a big enough event. There isn't too much homework. There isn't an important enough hockey game. There isn't too little time in the day. There aren't too many meetings. If I don't fulfill this calling, I'm not only failing my family, but I'm also failing my responsibilities before God.

Thank you to all my blogger friends for encouraging me with your posts. Thank you for helping me recognize my faults and pointing me in the direction I need to go. I'm thankful for this online community. I pray that you, too, will be encouraged to know you're not alone. I pray that you'll be nudged out of your comfort zone. Many of us well-intentioned moms stumble along the way. Just remember that all the compliments from others doesn't mean there aren't places to improve. It's easy to hide behind the best parts of life we choose to show each other on Facebook. I pray that, like me, you, too, will be convicted to get off your seat and make no excuses to read the Bible to your kids *every day.*

Let's hold each other accountable.

I share that with you to show that even those of us with the best intentions will fail at times. I also share it so you know you are not alone. If you ever feel like you should get the "Worst Mom of the Century" award, then sign the rest of us up with you. We've all been there and will likely be there again. We can't be perfect all the time, but we can encourage each other and hold each other accountable for our actions (or inaction). And when we mess up, we need to ask God and our families for forgiveness, brush ourselves off, get back up, and try again. Parenting is forever, after all, so giving up is not an option.

At All Times

In Ephesians 6:4, the Bible says to "bring [children] up in the training and instruction of the Lord" (HCSB). And in Deuteronomy 6:6–7 we read, "These words that I am giving you today are to be in your heart. Repeat them to your children. Talk about them when you sit in your house and when you walk along the road, when you lie down and when you get up" (HCSB). This is my goal—to teach my kids God's laws and biblical principles at all times so they will know how to live godly, balanced lives.

If you're not sure what to teach your kids or what kinds of rules and boundaries to set for them, I encourage you to dig into God's Word. I've found that I can't go wrong when I look to the Bible for advice on any topic, including parenting. I said earlier that I believe boundaries are the foundation for balance, and you really can't do any better than God's boundaries—for yourself or for your kids. When I look at God's laws, I try to see them in the same way I want my kids to see the rules I've set in place for them. He has rules for me because He loves me more than I can even imagine. All of those rules and commandments are for my good, not for my harm. Likewise, all of the rules and boundaries I set for my kids are for their good, because I love them more than life itself.

As a fifteen-year parenting veteran, I realize that though I've come a long way, I am far from having all the answers. I am constantly learning and readjusting my approach. But what I do know is that I can't give up. I have to keep fighting for my kids. Let's join together and determine to teach and guide our kids *at all times!*

CHAPTER 15

Do Something

*Then the righteous will answer Him, "Lord, when did
we see You hungry and feed You, or thirsty and give You
something to drink? When did we see You a stranger and
take You in, or without clothes and clothe You? . . ." And the
King will answer them, "I assure you: Whatever you did for
one of the least of these brothers of Mine, you did for Me."*
—MATTHEW 25:37–38, 40 (HCSB)

• • • • • • • • • • • • • • •

Imagine this if you will: A nine-year-old American boy
arrives on a Caribbean island with his family. Not long
after they get there, he finds himself in the company
of various other children he has never met. The little boy is
soon kicking around a ball with the other kids, playing games
with them, and basically just having a great time.

Did you imagine that little boy at a vacation resort with other middle- or upper-class travelers? If so, how about changing the background? Instead of a beachfront hotel, picture some one-room shacks with cracks between the boards and corrugated tin roofs. Rather than well-dressed, wealthy white children, imagine dark-skinned children who own nothing but the threadbare clothes on their backs.

Does that sound like a vacation to you? Maybe not, but that little nine-year-old boy loved every minute of it. Who is that boy? Well, he's my son. How did he get there? You'll find out if you keep reading!

You've probably noticed a theme throughout this book that many of the things I do in my life are a direct result of the way my parents raised me and the way they have lived their lives. That holds true in yet another part of my life— serving others. I have my mom to thank for the example of servanthood that she set before us as children and still sets today. When I was a kid, our home was like a revolving door. Mom was always inviting families to stay with us, whether they were hurting, sick, in need, or just because they needed a place to crash for a few nights. She always went above and beyond what was asked of her. She saw a need, and she filled it even when she had many other obligations.

During the *Full House* and *Growing Pains* days, we had weekly visits from terminally and chronically ill children through the Make-A-Wish and Starlight Foundations. I would always spend time with the kids by taking pictures and signing autographs and talking with them for a while. Since I was on set and working I usually didn't do much more than that, but that doesn't mean my mom didn't! She would quickly become fast friends with the families and take them to Disneyland or invite them to spend an extended day on the set of one or both of the shows or have them over to our house for dinner. Mom also always made sure there was a special place and time set aside for families with sick children to meet me at autograph signings and appearances when I traveled the country.

With her endless love for children and a heart for those in Africa, my mom laid a strong foundation for serving, helping, community, and charity. I pray I am half that example to my children.

I learned to serve others through my parents' example. The *reason* I serve, though, goes well beyond that. Jesus says that when we serve others—when we feed them, clothe them, visit them—we are really serving Him. And conversely, He also says that when we *don't* do those things for the people who need them, we are not only ignoring them, but we're also ignoring Him. I think that's a pretty big deal, and I think it's pretty obvious from those verses in Matthew 25 that God wants us to make serving others a priority.

Jesus also said, "It is more blessed to give than to receive" (Acts 20:35). I can tell you from experience that this is true. Though my reason for serving isn't because it makes me feel good, that is often the result. There's just something about helping others that gets me excited! I feel blessed to be able to donate money, but I feel just as good, if not better, when I'm investing in people's lives by talking with them, cooking and serving a meal to them, cleaning, packing up needed items, or just playing games with them.

Hear my heart when I say that I'm not trying to sound like a saint with a long list of worthy accomplishments, because I am certainly far from it. But I would like to share some acts of service my family and I do in the hope that it will inspire you to also place a priority on serving others. Before I do, I want to remind you how I said in the opening of this book that I don't believe balance is found by stripping down our priorities to the bare minimum, but rather by having well-balanced, careful priorities that reflect all the things God has created us to be and do. My story reflects that this is when balance is not only possible, but also most fulfilling!

Cultivating Hearts of Compassion

One of the charities I have supported for a long time and am passionate about is Compassion International. Through this organization, individuals and families can sponsor children around the world. A monthly donation goes toward food, shelter, schooling, and a host of other needs that the children might have. However, this program is not just about economic and physical needs. Compassion's mission is to meet children's spiritual and social needs as well. They are different from other aid organizations because instead of just relying on outsiders to go in and assess the needs of an area, they utilize the local church in these areas around the world. These churches are uniquely qualified to understand the real needs of the community and reach the children in poverty. They advocate for children, releasing them from spiritual, economic, social, and physical poverty, and enable them to become responsible, fulfilled Christian adults. To learn more about Compassion and sponsoring a child, visit www.compassion.com/candacecameronbure.

We first heard about Compassion through our church in Fort Lauderdale, which holds one of the largest percentages of sponsorships. Our family has been sponsoring three kids from Bangladesh for about nine years. Our sponsored children, Philimon, Sagorika, and Nikil, are the same ages as Natasha, Lev, and Maks. One of the great things about Compassion is that the sponsored kids can write to their sponsors, and we can write back. My hope was that my kids would become pen pals with our sponsored children, but unfortunately that still hasn't happened. They write letters once a year when I make them (oh, the joys of motherhood!), but I've primarily been the one who has done all of the writing. (I also write to the two kids in Uganda we sponsor through another organization. It's been a bit of a challenge keeping up!) Compassion also leads sponsor trips, where sponsors can actually go to the country where their children live and meet them. Putting real faces and places to the names on a piece of paper and photographs of children can make all the difference. Actually seeing the program work through the lives of real families opens up not only your eyes, but also your heart in ways that are unimaginable. My hope is to someday meet all of the children my family sponsors.

Though I haven't yet met Philimon, Sagorika, and Nikil, I did have the privilege of going on a Compassion trip to the Dominican Republic in the summer of 2011. When I was asked to go, I agreed to the trip, but I explained that it was important to me that my husband and kids went too. They had rarely included children on the sponsor trips, so it was a bit of uncharted territory for Compassion, but they agreed to allow my kids to go. Val and I weren't sure how our kids would respond to the sights, sounds, and smells of poverty in a developing nation and whether or not the circumstances would be overwhelming for them, but we were in agreement that it was important for them to experience life from another perspective. Val was much more familiar with what we were about to witness since he grew up in communist Russia, which was much different than the kids and me growing up in America.

I've had many parents ask if taking a nine-year-old to see such poverty is extreme, and my answer to that is, "This is how much of the world lives!" I believe it's my duty as a parent to expose my children as early as possible to the hardships of other people in order to grow compassion in their hearts. They will one day be the world changers! We must start as early as possible. Please understand that I wouldn't put my children in undue danger in order to expose them to such conditions, but if the circumstances are right and there is no risk to their health and lives I will take my children to as many places as possible in order to cultivate a heart for the poor, needy, orphans, and widows.

James 1:27 says, "Religion that is pure and undefiled before God, the Father, is this: *to visit orphans and widows in their affliction,* and to keep oneself unstained from the world" (emphasis mine). I don't believe that verse is just directed at adults. It is what He desires from all of us—children included. If they don't begin to see the world through compassionate eyes as children, what are the chances they will do so when they're adults?

So was the trip a success? As far as Val and I were concerned, yes! We were greatly moved by what we saw and learned in the Dominican Republic. God opened our eyes to the many needs there, but He also showed us how He is at work in amazing ways. He also taught us some valuable lessons about parenting and gave us some insights into the inner workings of our kids' lives and personalities.

Thirteen-year-old Natasha kept a journal about the trip, which she shared with friends and with Val and me. She wrote in great detail about our activities, and it was obvious that she really connected with the kids that were around her age, even though her life is so different than theirs. However, it was also plain to see that she was affected by those differences and by the living conditions of the people we visited. I think it's always a great thing for teenagers to have an opportunity to look outside of themselves and their relatively self-centered lives and see the needs of people living both in their own backyards and in other parts of the world.

Lev, my eleven-year-old with a sensitive heart, found himself sick to his stomach when we arrived at the communities where we were to spend our time in the Dominican. He stayed on the bus for portions of the trip instead of interacting with the kids and families we met because he was so overwhelmed by the conditions and what he saw and smelled. It was a lot for him to take in and I was very proud of him for making an effort to understand.

Nine-year-old Maks was the complete opposite of Lev . . . and he's the little boy in the story at the beginning of this chapter! Maks didn't see any barrier or difference between himself and the local kids. With his signature huge smile, he would ask if they wanted to kick a ball around, or play a game on my iPhone, or take pictures with our camera. In Maks's mind, he thought, *I'm a kid. You're a kid. Let's play!* It was amazing and it definitely surprised all of the people in our group.

So yes, I do believe that young children should be exposed to the conditions that kids around the world must live in day in and day out. And based on Maks's experience, Val and I—and many of the others on our trip—concluded that the younger our kids are when we expose them to the truths of poverty, the easier it will be for them to accept people who live in poverty and not be completely overwhelmed or negatively affected when they do. Young kids don't have the emotional, circumstantial, or social barriers that we start to develop as teens and adults that serve to separate people from different walks of life. They just see people as people, and they are eager to help and serve those who might not have what they have.

Supporting Worthy Causes

While Compassion International holds an important place in my heart, it is not the only charity that I'm involved with on an ongoing basis. I am also a huge supporter of Skip1.org and National House of Hope.

Do you realize that skipping something as small as your latte on the way to work on a daily, weekly, or even monthly basis can save a child's life? So many of us think we can only make an impact if we do something big, but the truth is that the accumulation of small things can add up to something much bigger than one large thing ever will. This is the mission behind Skip1.org. Their motto is, "Skip something. Feed a child," and was birthed by one of my dearest friends, Shelene Bryan.

What I love about Skip1 is that it's not just about a donation; it's also about denying ourselves something. Impoverished children don't have the choice to say, "No, thanks. I think I'll skip that meal today. I'm full," because most of them don't even get a meal. It's easy to give our money to charitable organizations when that money doesn't affect our daily lives, but it's very different when you're giving up something important to you. Sacrificing something also means that you don't have to have extra money to give back. Some of you college students have no more excuses!

Have you thought about skipping your lunch so that a kitchen could be built at an orphanage in Peru or clean water brought to a village in Uganda or homeless families fed right here in America? What would you have spent? Five, ten, twenty dollars? Seems like a small amount to give and a small sacrifice to make, but the impact is so great! So the next time you're at the grocery store and want to grab a pack of gum or a fashion magazine, how about skipping it? A car wash? A manicure? A new outfit? The possibilities are endless. Consider donating the money you would have spent on that item so that you can feed a child today. And the best part is that 100 percent of your donation goes to the acquisition and distribution of food and water projects worldwide! Just go to www.skip1.org.

A few years ago I was asked to be the national ambassador and representative of National House of Hope. Founded by Sara Trollinger, NHOH builds homes that help restore troubled teens and their families, resulting in these teens becoming solid citizens and effective, contributing members of society. As the mom of two teenagers, I can see the need and value in this program.

NHOH has more than thirty homes in the United States, and their immediate goal is to have one in every state. I've not only had the privilege of meeting many of the teens staying at Houses of Hope and seeing their inspiring progress, but I've also gleaned much wisdom and support from this organization as a parent. I'm so very grateful for what NHOH does and I encourage you to get involved. Check them out at www.nationalhouseofhope.org.

While these are not the only organizations I support, they are the ones I am most focused on at this point in my life. I have been involved with many others throughout the years, such as The Children's Hunger Fund, Scleroderma Research Foundation, World Vision, Harvest Home, Operation Smile, and many more. Sometimes my involvement is monetary, but more often I donate my time. I believe that giving of myself has everlasting value, and I hope you do too.

A Family Affair

Some of my charity work is done on my own, but much of it is done with my family. I think it's important for families to serve others together. It helps to tighten your bond as a family, and it also helps out with balancing and prioritizing. If family and service are both priorities, combining the two just makes both more purposeful.

One of our family's newest service traditions is serving at a homeless shelter on Christmas mornings. Together with a few friends and family, we find a small shelter that allows us to come in and cook for their guests, which range from thirty to sixty people. This past Christmas, Val cooked eggs, bacon, and sausage while the rest of us—including the kids—set out fruit, muffins, breads, waffles, cereals, coffee, and juices. After all of the guests filled their plates, we all sat down and ate together. We listened to our new homeless friends' stories, as they explained how they ended up there and how they are putting the pieces of their lives back together. I brought along Bible gift boxes that included a worship CD, and many of the folks were delighted to take one. We also passed out fun fuzzy socks to each person, for which they were very thankful!

I try to plant seeds in my kids that will help them think of special ways they can help others. I encourage them to think about what matters most to them. What types of needs tug at their heartstrings? If they don't have an answer, I help them out by providing a few options where they could donate their time, energy, and allowance, and then I let them choose which one they most want to do. For example, you might suggest that they "skip" a few birthday presents by asking family members to give them the cash they would have spent on a present so they can turn around and make a donation to Skip1.org. Allowing your children to be a part of the giving back process allows them to experience the feeling of giving rather than having others do it for them. Or perhaps you could list out some of your favorite nonprofits and let the child choose where he would like to donate some of his time one Saturday morning. You know your kids' interests and hearts, so encourage them to use those things to serve others.

If your kids are involved in sports, you might want to consider getting your child's team affiliated with a nonprofit organization and raising funds by donating money for each point or win. For our hockey teams, we have a dollar bucket that gets passed around for every goal the team scores. Some of that money goes back into team funds, but portions of it are donated to charity. Sometimes we will collect more than one hundred dollars in one game! In October, most of the boys wrap their hockey sticks with pink tape in honor of Breast Cancer Awareness month and parents donate a specific amount per goal for their child or team for the month.

My kids are also involved in service projects through their school. They routinely work with Soldiers' Angels, packing up needed items for our troops and sending encouraging thank-you notes to them. We also serve at the area veterans' center and a local homeless pregnancy house, where we'll paint, garden, or help fix anything that needs working on. One of the projects my kids do several times a year is collect fresh, canned, and packaged food for the local food bank and then help the bank sort and box up the food to be delivered to shelters. Most schools, whether they're public, private, or home school co-ops, welcome children's efforts for charity. If your kids' school isn't involved in community service, I challenge you and your kids to come up with an idea and plan and present it to a teacher or administrator. I would guess that they won't turn you down!

In addition, our church is affiliated with the Union Rescue Mission in downtown Los Angeles. Each year we put on a carnival for the resident families and host a water day, complete with water balloons, a water slide, and plenty of food. And one of my favorite things to do each November is to pack up a few shoes boxes with small gifts that are sent off to Operation Christmas Child and distributed to needy children throughout the world.

A Legacy of Giving

Back in chapter 1, I shared this verse with you: "Train up a child in the way he should go; even when he is old he will not depart from it" (Prov. 22:6). When I look at the legacy of serving others in my family, I can once again see the truth in this ancient proverb. My parents set an example for what I do as a person, but also for what I do as a parent. They "trained me up" to serve others, and then as an adult I followed in their footsteps by serving others, and now I also set that example for my own kids. It is my hope that my kids will continue this trend with their own children someday.

I am doing everything I can in order to show my kids the importance of serving. I realize that not all of you will be able to serve in the same ways I do or to give your kids the same kinds of experiences that I have given mine. You might not be able to take your children on a mission trip to another country. You may not have the financial resources to give much money. But what you do have is time, skills, and talents. We all have equal amounts of those, and it is up to us to figure out how and where to use them. In my experience, service often boils down to valuing other human beings and showing love to those who are often neglected. That is something that we can do for free and by doing so we are able to bring meaningful balance to the priorities of family, faith, and service.

As adults and parents, I believe we need to set the example of service for the kids in our lives—whether they're our own kids or someone else's. If we're serving, we're acting as role models, and the children we influence will want to do what we do and therefore will do it with a happy heart. And who knows? Maybe one of these days, they'll even start serving us!

CHAPTER 16

When Life's Got You Stressed

And whatever you ask in prayer, you will receive,
if you have faith.

—MATTHEW 21:22

• • • • • • • • • • • • •

When you're in the worst of times, you're always remembering the best of times. You ask yourself, *Where did it go wrong?* You wonder how you got to where you are and how to get back to the good old days. Sometimes it's as easy as answering a few questions to get you rerouted and on the right track. Other times, things have changed too much and it's not as simple as doing what you did before. Circumstances might not allow it. You read all of these principles for living a balanced life, and you think, *It's just too much to handle. Things are too far out of control. What do I do?*

Do what I do: have a good cry, take some deep breaths, and *pray!* Prayer is often the only thing that keeps me hanging on when something is wrong or in a season of imbalance. Oh, I've been there. I'm actually going through it right now, and it's only getting harder. It's not that I'm trying any less; in fact, I'm trying more, praying harder, and trusting in the Lord more than ever. But things aren't changing and I'm getting weary. At least I know I'm not alone. Some of you have been there or are in it right now. I have friends going through it and it's comforting to know I'm not the first person nor will I be the last person to feel this way.

Some people gain faith in their trials while other people question it or lose it. For me, I have my faith, I'm keeping it, and I'm hanging on to the words and promises God has given me. Some days it's hard to remember why I should be happy beyond my circumstances, until I recall Psalm 51:12: "Restore the joy of Your salvation to me, and give me a willing spirit" (HCSB). I find my joy in the Lord alone, because of His love and sacrifice for me. I don't always *feel* like I can find my joy in that, but I turn to Scripture throughout the day so I can remind myself of that truth. I find that it takes a combination of prayer and God's Word to keep me on the right path. Some days Psalm 51:12 penetrates my heart more than others, and I love when it does. And on the days I don't feel any connection to God, I say it in truth, not in feeling, knowing that my emotions will change from day to day and it will be restored to me. But regardless of whether I feel joyful or feel like praying, I keep doing it, and I keep believing. Matthew 21:22 says, "And whatever you ask in prayer, you will receive, if you have faith." There is a vital link between faith and prayer, and I have to hold tight to that truth.

A Beautiful Partnership

My prayer life went on steroids two years ago and I feel like I finally have a grasp of what it's like to *really* pray. I know I'm just getting started on this prayer journey, but it's been quite a ride so far. God time has always been a difficult thing in my life because I never felt like I had a good example of what that looked like. "Go pray," friends would say, or "Just spend time with God about it." Okay, I'd love to! But what does that really mean? How do I do that? Even when I would be doing my homework for Bible study, and it said to talk to God about xyz, I just didn't know what exactly I was supposed to do. I knew I could talk to God at any time, any place, with or without my eyes closed. Talking to God is like talking to a friend, so you just talk, out loud or in your mind. He hears it all. So I would do that, but I would feel like it was a one-sided conversation. "Read your Bible. That's how He answers back," people would say. So I'd read my Bible. Sometimes it was random, but most of the time it was whatever I was studying in small group. However, those were times of specific prayer, and not necessarily related to my personal "prayer time," so I felt like there was a disconnect. Basically, I wanted a step-by-step guide on how to pray, how to hear God answering those prayers, and how to get my prayer life boosted to the next level.

My friend Stacy in Ohio e-mailed me more than two years ago and asked if I would like to be her prayer partner. Prayer partner? That sounded big. I didn't know exactly what it would entail and what kind of commitment it would mean. I am brilliant at overextending myself and the last thing I needed to do was to make a commitment I couldn't keep. And I certainly didn't want to commit to someone's prayer needs and then bail on her! How awful would that be? So I told Stacy I'd have to pray about it.

For a few weeks I really did pray about it and I felt God saying, "Here you go. Take this step and commit. It's putting you in a place where you can't back out because it's not just you who depends on it; her prayers are in your hands." At the same time, I realized that my prayers would be in her hands. Stacy would also be committing to pray for me, and

I knew she would uphold her end of the partnership. I also knew I could trust her with my most personal information, which was a pretty big deal. So I felt like God wanted me to do it and I agreed. Which, just goes to show (again!) that balance isn't necessarily about cutting things out of our lives, but rather being led to invest in the right things.

Because I'm not much of a phone talker, e-mail was a better choice for us, so we decided to write out our requests to each other every week. And, because they were being written down, it was an easy way of keeping track of prayers that God answered, as well as seeing the things about which we needed to keep praying.

The results have been amazing. The way we've prayed has been amazing. The detail in which we write out our requests and pray for one another has opened my eyes to just how small I've considered God to be. But He's big—*He can move mountains* big, *He can heal anyone* big, *He can fix anything* big, *He can restore* big. And my amazement isn't a result of God answering all of my prayer requests, because He hasn't . . . yet. But seeing Stacy's prayers being answered has been so encouraging to me that it keeps me coming back for more prayer. A day without prayer is a day wasted of an opportunity to see God's hand in my life. I just can't go a day without it any more.

I've also experienced the flip side of a strong prayer life, which is spiritual attacks. I haven't had such a hard season in all my life and I have no doubt it's due to the enemy being on double duty, throwing flaming darts my way to discourage me, make me feel like God's not with me, and ultimately to try to get me to stop praying for miracles. But I'm on to Satan, and he's not going to win. I know God's power, and not just because of what I've seen Him do in other people's lives, but also because of what He has done in my own.

Burnt Popcorn

When Lev was four years old we were told he had cholesteatoma in his right ear. Without surgeries, the condition is fatal. It deteriorates anything with which it comes into contact, and Lev's hearing had already suffered. He had lost two and a half hearing bones, leaving him with less than 20 percent auditory function in that ear. After his first surgery, we had been told he'd need a second surgery to make sure not one cell had been left. Otherwise, like cancer, it would just grow back and spread.

Lev's second surgery went well and the doctor believed everything was gone, but only the CT scan would prove that, and the test was scheduled for the following week. For the first time in our lives, Val and I decided to fast and pray for twenty-four hours the day before the scan until the following evening after it took place. We wanted the best possible results and sensed that this was the biggest thing we could do in an effort to show God that we had faith He could heal our son through the doctor's hands and His healing power.

I didn't know how long we would have to wait for the results, so as Val and Lev drove home from his appointment, I called the doctor's office. I explained that my son had just had his CT scan and we had the disk in hand. I asked how long it would take the doctor to have a look and let us know the results. The receptionist told me that the doctor was actually leaving that evening for Europe and wouldn't be back in the office for four weeks. Four weeks? I wouldn't know whether or not Lev was in the clear for four weeks? This just wasn't happening. So I begged and I pleaded for the doctor to look at the results *that day* before he left. Mama bear was upright on her hind legs, letting out a roar of protection for her baby cub.

The receptionist was sympathetic, but there wasn't anything she could do. The doctor's schedule was full, and besides, he was only going be there for another two hours. I asked if there was any way she would squeeze me in if I drove down right then. She said it was highly unlikely, but I was more than welcome to try. The doctor's office was a full hour's drive away, so as soon as the boys got home, I grabbed the disk from them and drove into the heart of Miami. I prayed out loud during the entire drive, asking God for a miracle. I asked that He would make a way for me to see the doctor and personally hand him the disk. If nothing else, I hoped he'd take a look at it on his flight to Europe and call us from there.

I literally prayed without ceasing. I didn't stop. I called on the name of the Lord, pleading for Him to do something big. I asked Him to part the traffic for me, I asked Him for a close parking spot, and I asked Him to somehow get me face-to-face with Lev's surgeon.

As I walked over to the Otology building from the hospital parking structure I noticed that there were crowds of people waiting outside the double doors and no one was going in. I walked up to the security officer and asked what was going on. "The fire alarm went off. The building has been evacuated." I immediately felt like God was doing something just for me. Could it be? After fifteen minutes, security told everyone it was a false alarm and it was clear to go back in. I jammed into the elevator as quickly as I could and went to our doctor's floor. When I got off, there wasn't a soul in sight, so I assumed I was the first one back. I kept praying, "God, please let me see the doctor when he comes up the elevator!"

I waited a few more minutes in the waiting room and then decided to open the door and walk by the examining rooms to see if I could find a nurse or receptionist. I heard two voices. Great! Those two voices were men and then I heard, "Okay, have a great trip to Europe. We'll see you when you get back." And as soon as his sentence finished, I saw Lev's doctor turn the corner. There I was, face-to-face with the man I had come to see. As quickly and politely as I could, I explained the situation. He patiently listened to me, looked around, and said, "Well, it seems as if no one is back from the fire alarm scare, so I don't have any patients waiting. Why don't you come into my office and I'll take a look at the CD right now?" The hair on my arms stood right up!

We sat down together at his computer and after looking through the images for several minutes, he declared Lev perfectly healthy and clear of any cholesteatoma. Lev wouldn't need to be checked again for another year, and the next appointment would just be an annual, precautionary measure. Chills went up and down my body. I couldn't believe I was experiencing a real miracle. Not only were our son's results what we had been praying for, but I was blown away that God had used burnt popcorn in a microwave to clear an entire office building so that I could meet face-to-face with my doctor and have him read the results to me at that very moment. There was no doubt in my mind that our prayers and fasting were directly related to the outcome of that situation.

Pray Big

As miraculous as my prayers were that day, I've also seen God answer many of my prayers on a much smaller scale. I've learned to pray very specific and detailed prayers so that I can see the hand of God working and know that it's Him answering and not just coincidence or fate, as some might believe. Many of us think God doesn't answer our prayers, but I would argue that either the prayers are too vague or we don't really know what we're praying for in the first place.

If your marriage is suffering, instead of just asking God to fix your marriage, ask God to change your heart and to open your eyes to the details of what you need to change that would cause your husband to act more loving, respectful, or emotional with you. Ask Him to help you be more acceptable to criticism without being defensive, if that's something you have trouble with. Ask Him to help you find your joy even when your circumstances don't lend themselves to exciting things. If you're struggling with your children, don't just ask God to bless your parenting or kids, ask Him with details. Is your son's attitude out of control? Is your daughter struggling in school? Is your toddler having nightmares and scared to sleep? There is no request too big or too small. If we fail to ask God in great detail, we'll miss out on great blessings. God wants a willing heart. It's time to get real with God.

You don't have to take my word for it when it comes to the importance and effectiveness of prayer. God's Word talks about it over and over.

- "This is the confidence we have in approaching God: that if we ask anything according to his will, he hears us. And if we know that he hears us—whatever we ask—we know that we have what we asked of him" (1 John 5:14–15 NIV).
- "If any of you lacks wisdom, you should ask God, who gives generously to all without finding fault, and it will be given to you. But when you ask, you must believe and not doubt, because the one who doubts is like a wave of the sea, blown and tossed by the wind" (James 1:5–6 NIV).
- "You do not have because you do not ask God" (James 4:2 NIV).
- "I call on you, my God, for you will answer me; turn your ear to me and hear my prayer" (Ps. 17:6 NIV).

A Prayer for You

What does spending time with God look like? It's different for everyone, but there are plenty of resources out there to help you figure it out. Becky Tirabassi's book *Let Prayer Change Your Life* gave me an almost step-by-step guide to follow. That doesn't mean there is one right way to pray, because there's not, but I needed someone to spell it out for me and get me to a starting place. *The Circle Maker* by Mark Batterson had the biggest impact on my prayer life in 2012. My prayer life has evolved into what works best for me and my schedule and has come to a place where I'm finally comfortable and know what spending time with God means and looks like. This is also my prayer for you.

Whether you're currently in a good place or tough place spiritually, I hope you will keep prayer a priority. I know from experience that it's not easy, but without it, we won't have a fighting chance. Prayer brings us closer to God, and no matter how many principles we follow—biblical or not— to try to live a life of balance and purpose, it ultimately all amounts to nothing without a relationship with God and with His Son, Jesus.

I want to leave you with a prayer *you* can pray as you finish up this book. Feel free to change it up or add to it. Just make sure it comes from your heart!

Lord,

I praise You because I am fearfully and wonderfully made; Your works are wonderful, I know that full well. Thank You for creating me as a unique and special person. It amazes me that there is not another human with the exact same blueprint. You have ordained all the days of my life even before one of them came to be. I surrender wholly to You and ask You to guide me each step of the way.

God, help me zero in on my priorities. Show me what is most important and help me juggle the day-to-day tasks that need to get done. I understand that if I prioritize the macro, managing the micro will be easier and not so overwhelming. I also know that I need not compare myself to others. What will work best for me and my family will look different than what works for others.

Show me how You should come first in my life. Help me put it into practice with prayer, reading my Bible, and befriending like-minded women who will encourage me. Bring those relationships into my life and help me nurture the ones I already have.

Help me to remember that in order to balance my life, there are four areas I need to pay close attention to: my physical health, emotional health, mental health, and spiritual health. I know that my emotional and mental health are closely connected to my spiritual health, so help me not to neglect my relationship with You; for the joy of You, Lord, is my strength.

Remind me to put others' needs before my own, especially my family. It's easy to treat the people closest to me the worst because of routine or comfort levels. But reveal them to me in a new light—Your light. Help me see them the way You do. I want to care for the poor and be an example to my children, family, and friends with a heart that overflows with compassion. Bring to my mind creative ways I can be of service to others.

Balancing it all isn't easy, but I know that I can do all things through Your Son, Jesus Christ, who strengthens me.

Finally, whatever is true, whatever is noble, whatever is right, whatever is pure, whatever is lovely, whatever is admirable—if anything is excellent or praiseworthy—help me to think about such things and put them into practice. Help me to remember that when I do this, You—the God of peace—will be with me.

Amen.

APPENDIX

Recommended Resources

Charities

Skip1.org: www.skip1.org

Compassion International: www.compassion.com/candace
cameronbure

National House of Hope: www.nationalhouseofhope.org

Make-A-Wish Foundation: www.wish.org

Starlight Foundation: www.starlight.org

Union Rescue Mission: www.urm.org

Harvest Home: www.theharvesthome.net

Claris Health: www.clarishealth.org

Soldiers' Angels: www.soldiersangels.org

Operation Christmas Child: www.samaritanspurse.org

Scleroderma Research Foundation: www.srfcure.org

Operation Smile: www.operationsmile.org
Children's Hunger Fund: www.chfus.org
World Vision: www.worldvision.org

Books

Brokenness by Nancy Leigh DeMoss
Let Prayer Change Your Life by Becky Tirabassi
Love and Respect by Dr. Emerson Eggerichs
The 5 Love Languages by Gary Chapman
The Circle Maker by Mark Batterson
The Excellent Wife by Martha Peace
The Way of the Master by Ray Comfort
On Becoming Baby Wise by Gary Ezzo
Real Marriage by Mark and Grace Driscoll
Shepherding a Child's Heart by Tedd Tripp

Also Available

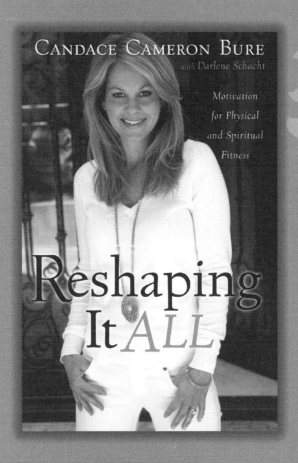

CANDACE CAMERON BURE
with Darlene Schacht

Motivation
for Physical
and Spiritual
Fitness

Reshaping
It ALL